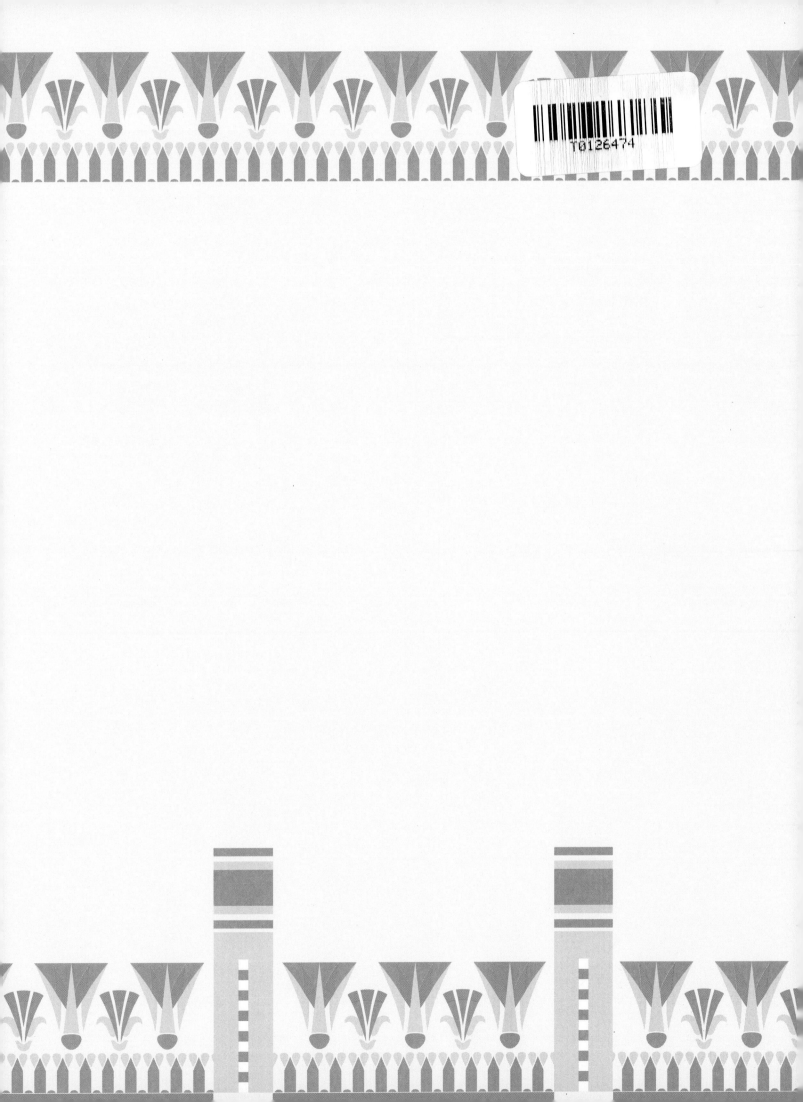

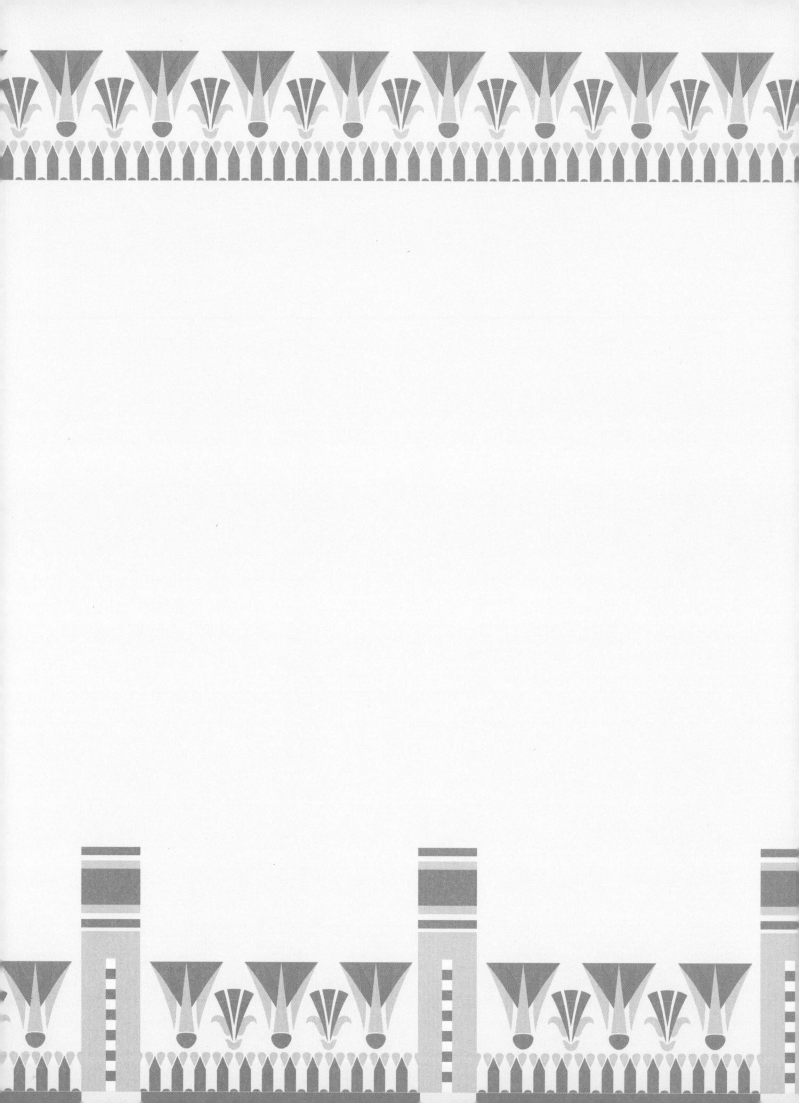

ANCIENT EGYPT

ANCIENT

EGYPT

TREASURES FROM THE
COLLECTION OF
THE ORIENTAL INSTITUTE
UNIVERSITY OF CHICAGO

Emily Teeter

This book is for Joe

Oriental Institute Museum Publications no. 23

Published by The Oriental Institute of The University of Chicago.
1155 East 58th Street, Chicago, IL 60637 USA
www-oi.uchicago.edu

Edited by Emily Napolitano and Thomas Urban
Designed and typeset by Joan Sommers Design, Chicago
Printed and bound by Asia Pacific Offset
Printed in China

Photo credits: Unless otherwise indicated, all photographs are by Oriental Institute staff photographers. Introduction: fig. 1. un-attributed newspaper photograph, from the scrapbook of Frances Hart Breasted; fig. 4. Chicago Architectural Photographing Company; fig. 5. Lloyd DeGrane. Object nos. 1–3, 8–9, 11–12, 14, 17–18, 21, 24, 29a-b–35, 37, 43, 46–48, 50–62 Jean M. Grant, The Oriental Institute; no. 13 Jean M. Grant and Joe Denov, The Oriental Institute; no. 7 (10628, 10641, 10642) Bruce White; no. 36 Peter Brenner

ISBN 1-88592-325-2
Library of Congress Control No. 2003104249

Cover: Nen-Khefet-Ka and Nefer-shemes (no. 8)
Title page: Musician (no. 7)
End sheets: Design based on ceiling decoration, Oriental Institute Museum
Back cover: Stela of Djed-khonsu-iw-es-ankh (no. 37)

THIS PUBLICATION WAS MADE POSSIBLE
BY THE GENEROSITY OF THE WOMEN'S BOARD
OF THE UNIVERSITY OF CHICAGO

CONTENTS

PREFACE

THIS BOOK PRESENTS ancient Egyptian artifacts from the collection of the Oriental Institute Museum of the University of Chicago. The Museum's holdings are very rich but, ironically, few of the more than 25,000 pieces from the Nile Valley are well known outside of academic circles, as they have been published only in scholarly journals. Only a few objects from the collection—primarily those which have been included in traveling exhibits—have been illustrated and discussed in catalogues accessible to scholars and the public alike. The extent to which the collection is unknown is attested by the number of very significant objects in this book for which there is simply no publication history.

The choice of objects to be included in this volume was based on the some-what idiosyncratic choices of the author. In the attempt to give the widest view of the collection, the selection was not restricted to regal statues and reliefs. Written documents, grooming tools, decorative tiles, clothing, and figurines—objects that are rarely illustrated elsewhere—were also included. Esthetic value was not the overriding element in inclusion, cultural significance was perhaps a more important factor. The broad variety of artifacts will, it is hoped, give the reader an appreciation of the range and depth of treasures of the Oriental Institute collection and the variety of Egyptian artifacts overall.

The Egyptian collection of the Oriental Institute cannot be disassociated from the personality of its founder, James Henry Breasted. The introductory essay on the history of the collection attempts to show the influence of this giant of Egyptology and how his academic policies and the colorful history of his Institute shaped the Egyptian collection.

Emily Teeter
Research Associate
Curator of Egyptian and Nubian Antiquities
The Oriental Institute

ACKNOWLEDGMENTS

ALTHOUGH THE ORIENTAL INSTITUTE has long been recognized to be among the world's leaders in the field of ancient Near Eastern studies, the holdings of its museum are not widely known to the public. It is hoped that this book, and others to follow, will bring the richness of the collection to the attention of scholars and the general public alike.

The need for illustrated catalogues of significant objects in the collection has long been acknowledged. The complete renovation of the museum, which was initiated in 1996, provided the impetus to initiate the project. A generous grant from the Women's Board of the University of Chicago in 1998 enabled the Oriental Institute Museum finally to realize this publication series. This grant is a reflection of the Women Board's concern that the university community, schools, and the more general arts and humanities communities be exposed to the holdings of the museum and to the highly significant role that the University of Chicago has played in the recovery of the languages, history, and culture of the ancient Near East. I express my sincere thanks to Mrs. Diana King, then Chairman of the Women's Board, and Mrs. Jetta Jones, Chairman of the 1998 Projects Committee, as well as to the entire Women's Board for their confidence and generous support of the research projects of the Oriental Institute.

The author wishes to extend thanks to Gil Stein, Director of the Oriental Institute, for bringing this project to fruition. I also thank former Director Gene Gragg, and Karen Wilson, Director of the Oriental Institute Museum, for facilitating the initial stages of the project. I thank my immediate colleagues Peter Dorman, Janet Johnson, W. Raymond Johnson, Robert Ritner, Robert Biggs, Thomas Urban and Thomas Holland, and also Ronald Leprohon, Richard Fazzini, Edna Russmann, and T. G. Wilfong who gave useful advice. Oriental Institute Archivist John Larson assisted with the selection of images. Much of the photography is the work of Jean Grant, photographer at the Oriental Institute. Emily Napolitano undertook the final copy editing.

Loyal volunteers of the Oriental Institute assisted in many ways. Janet Kessler kindly made numerous suggestions regarding the text, Peggy Grant checked bibliographic references, Richard Harter scanned images, and Masako Matsumota checked object dimensions. I thank them all for their assistance and for their friendship.

I extend special thanks for the on-going support of Gretel Braidwood, Executive Secretary of the Women's Board, for her unflagging and consistent support of the Oriental Institute.

A History of the Egyptian Collection

FIGURE 1.
View of the south hall of Haskell
Museum in 1896 showing the exhibit
arranged by Breasted. At this time,
the collections consisted primarily
of plaster casts and small objects
purchased by Breasted on his honeymoon trip.

THE COLLECTION OF MORE THAN 25,000 ancient Egyptian artifacts
housed at the Oriental Institute of the University of Chicago is among the most
important in North America. The objects came to the American Midwest through
the carefully orchestrated plans and the sheer force of personality of men who
reflected the optimism and spirit characteristic of the advent of the 20th century—
John D. Rockefeller, Sr., his son John D. Rockefeller, Jr., William Rainey Harper,
and James Henry Breasted. In two generations these men created a world-renowned
university, museum, and research institute devoted to the study of ancient Egypt and
the Near East which was to shape the disciplines of Egyptology and ancient Near
Eastern studies.

John D. Rockefeller, Sr., provided generous financial grants for the foundation
of the University of Chicago in 1890. Working with the Board of Trustees he began
the search for a president for the fledgling university. Their candidate was William
Rainey Harper, a Semitic scholar at Yale University, whom Rockefeller wooed to the
Midwest with promises of financial aid to establish an Institute of Hebrew and an
American Institute of Sacred Literature.[1] As Rockefeller wrote to the prospective
president, "I agree with the Board of Trustees that you are the man for president,
and if you will take it, I shall expect great results."[2] Rockefeller was not to be disappointed. Harper accepted the position as the first president of the University of
Chicago and head of the Department of Semitic Languages, and he began assem-
bling a core of scholars who would distinguish the university. He persuaded his
brother, Robert Francis Harper, a scholar of Akkadian, to follow him to Chicago.
In 1890, while still at Yale, President Harper met graduate student James Henry

Breasted, who was to be crucial to the future of Egyptology in Chicago, and indeed the world. Before coming to Yale, Breasted had studied for a career in the ministry. However, while studying Hebrew he became disillusioned by the tremendous discrepencies between the original Hebrew texts of the Old Testament and their translation in the King James Bible. Breasted professed his horror at the lack of fidelity to the original texts writing, "I could never be satisfied to preach on the basis of texts I know to be full of mistranslation."[3] This fundamental lesson in the importance of making accurate translations of ancient texts from which history could be written was to define his career and the direction of scholarly work at the University of Chicago. Harper encouraged Breasted to undertake graduate studies in Egyptology in Berlin, then the world leader in the discipline, promising him, "Breasted, if you will go to Germany and get the best possible scientific equipment, no matter if it takes you five years, I will give you the professorship of Egyptology in the new University of Chicago!"[4]

In 1894 Breasted graduated from Berlin with honors and became the first American to receive a Ph.D. in Egyptology. His dissertation, prepared (in Latin!) under the supervision of Adolph Erman and Eduard Meyer, dealt with monotheistic hymns of the Amarna Period. While studying in Berlin he visited museum collections throughout Europe making painstakingly accurate copies of hieroglyphic texts that appeared on artifacts.

That same year, Breasted and his American-born wife, Frances Hart, traveled to Egypt on their honeymoon. This was Breasted's first opportunity to visit the Nile Valley, and his wife's diaries suggest that the monuments were indeed a distraction: "Tuesday [January 15, 1895] we spent over here at the north tombs [of Tell el Amarna]— I reading and husband as usual, copying."

Harper gave Breasted $500 to buy objects for the University of Chicago with the directive that he should rely upon the generosity of dealers as much as possible and return with the maximum number of artifacts and the most change. Breasted bought modest items such as mummified animals, ushebtis, amulets, and fragments of statues and reliefs, perhaps being hesitant to make commitments to more significant objects. His wife's diaries comment that Breasted spent a day dickering over the price of four mummies. He then hired camels to carry them to the river where they were loaded "right into our bedrooms and [we] did not lose any sleep."

The honeymoon trip was also his first opportunity to examine the wealth of hieroglyphic inscriptions that covered the temples and tombs. He was shocked by the inaccuracies of the published versions of the texts and vowed, "I am now laying plans to copy not merely the historical, but *all* the inscriptions of Egypt and publish them."[5]

In 1896, the fledgling collection of artifacts at the University of Chicago was moved from storage space in the basement of the Walker Museum into the Haskell Oriental Museum. This building, named in honor of the late husband of Caroline E. Haskell, was established with the mission of making "possible the broader and deeper study of the world's sacred scriptures . . ."[6] Harper served as the first Director of the museum, and Breasted as the Assistant Director. The collection consisted mainly of "a few plaster cast reproductions and a small group of exhibit cases containing the little collection of antiquities" that Breasted brought back from his honeymoon trip (fig. 1). He commented that there were no books, no students, and a very low salary. This last shortcoming motivated him to undertake a series of ambitious lecture tours that served to fine-tune his ability to captivate the public with scholarly, yet entertaining, talks on ancient Egypt. His talks were warmly received. As reported in a local paper: "His subjects are explained and fastened better in memory by being illustrated with beautiful stereopticon views . . ." and "he handles his subjects with a masterly hand, not stopping his limitless flow until his hour is more than gone."[7]

Breasted was disappointed that, due to the influence of Robert Francis Harper, the first field expedition of the Department of Semitic Studies was dedicated to the excavation of Bismaya (ancient Adab) in Iraq rather than to work in Egypt. However, after the premature curtailment of the Bismaya expedition, the balance of the funding for the expedition was made available for the First Epigraphic Survey—dedicated to copying the inscriptions in the Nile Valley. In two seasons (1905–06, 1906–07), Breasted, accompanied by an assistant and a photographer, took over 1,100 glass plate negatives (carried on camel back and in a small boat through the treacherous cataracts of the Nile), which are still valuable records of monuments south of the First Cataract. During this grueling expedition, Breasted refined his technique of copying inscriptions that developed into the "Chicago House" method that is still used today.

The constant financial strain of Breasted's modest salary motivated him to lecture constantly and to write popular books. His *History of Egypt*, published in 1906, was ultimately translated into many languages as well as Braille. Part of his quest to educate the public about the ancient Near East provided the impetus to produce the text book *Ancient Times* (1916), which Breasted professed to have hated writing. However, this book provided the key to Breasted's future success, for Mrs. John D. Rockefeller, Jr., read the book to her children at night, impressing her husband with Breasted's ability to communicate with the public.

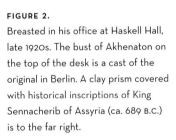

FIGURE 2.
Breasted in his office at Haskell Hall, late 1920s. The bust of Akhenaton on the top of the desk is a cast of the original in Berlin. A clay prism covered with historical inscriptions of King Sennacherib of Assyria (ca. 689 B.C.) is to the far right.

In 1919, Breasted applied to the Rockefeller-supported General Education Fund to fund a survey of the Near East and to establish a research center at the University of Chicago. That institution, christened the Oriental Institute in 1919, was envisioned as a "research laboratory for the investigation of the early human career"[8] which would trace man's "progress" from the most ancient days of the Near East. An important feature of the Oriental Institute was its museum. It exhibited Breasted's modest purchases, as well as the many artifacts received as a result of the University's financial support of the excavations of London's Egypt Exploration Fund (later the Egypt Exploration Society) and Egyptian Research Account (fig. 3).

The Egypt Exploration Fund and Egyptian Research Account continued to be the conduit for most new acquisitions of Egyptian material until 1919–20 when Breasted (later joined by colleagues D. D. Luckinbill, A. W. Shelton, William F. Edgerton, and Ludlow Bull), traveled through Egypt and on to the Near East scouting possible excavation sites and making significant purchases of antiquities. Breasted commented that this was an ideal time to add to the collections: "The situation is this. . . There is a body of material here in Cairo, which will never be available again . . ."[9] He also

FIGURE 3.
View of the north hall of Haskell Museum in 1922. The exhibit was composed primarily of objects from the excavations of the Egypt Exploration Fund and the British School of Archaeology in Egypt, and of objects purchased by Breasted in 1919-20. Catalogue numbers 35, 38, and 52 are visible in the background.

FIGURE 4.

View of the Oriental Institute Egyptian gallery, 1935. The ceiling is stenciled with Egyptian-inspired designs and the light fixtures imitate a type of ancient pottery. The end of the hall is dominated by a colossal winged bull from the Oriental Institute's excavations at Khorsabad, Iraq.

bought for the Art Institute of Chicago, spending more than $15,000 on their behalf and acquiring some of the key Egyptian pieces of that collection. The following year he was appointed honorary curator of Egyptian Art at the Art Institute of Chicago.

Following the 1919–20 survey of Egypt, the Oriental Institute concluded an agreement with the Egyptian government to start work at the temple of Ramesses III at Medinet Habu in Luxor. This project was approached on two fronts. The Architectural Survey (1926–33), under the direction of Uvo Hölscher, cleared the temple and documented its architectural history and the artifacts from the precinct, while the Epigraphic Survey (1924–), initially under Harold Nelson, copied the reliefs and inscriptions on its walls.

The 1930s saw tremendous growth in the collections of the Oriental Institute. The excavations at Medinet Habu resulted in the addition of approximately 8,000 objects (see nos. 23, 29, 30, 33, 36, 40, 62). This excavation was conducted at the same time as the Institute's work at Megiddo (Israel), Persepolis (Iran), the Amuq (Turkey), and Khorsabad and Khafajah (Iraq), resulting in a veritable flood of antiquities to Chicago. Between 1929 and 1939, the number of museum holdings doubled. The growing collection was housed in a building constructed exclusively for the Oriental Institute, and again funded by the generosity of John D. Rockefeller, Jr. When the building opened in 1931, it included five galleries, one of which was devoted to Egypt (fig. 4).

With the conclusion of the excavations of Medinet Habu in 1933, the death of Breasted in 1935, reduced funding, and the reduction of divisions of antiquities by

FIGURE 5.

View of the Joseph and Mary Grimshaw Egyptian Gallery in 1999.

Egypt, the growth of the Egyptian collection slowed considerably. Yet, significant acquisitions were made in the 1950s (see nos. 41, 47) and objects continued to be added through the excavation of Roman and medieval Quseir on the Red Sea Coast (1978–82) and the 1960–68 UNESCO-sponsored excavations in Nubia. In addition, important objects have been added to the collection through individual gifts (see nos. 17, 56), or by exchange with other institutions (see no. 18).

The first Curator of the Oriental Institute Museum, Pinhas Delougaz, was responsible for the reorganization of the museum storage and exhibit areas. His Research Assistants, Miriam Lichtheim (who held the position 1944–48 and 1949–51) and Helene J. Kantor (1945–48, and later Professor at the Oriental Institute), undertook a virtual "excavation" of the basement, and published important studies on pieces in the collection.[10] In 1969, Gustavus Swift was appointed the first full-time non-faculty curator. Although there were minor modifications made to the appearance of the Egyptian gallery over the next 25 years, the need to install climate control systems to the exhibit and storage areas provided the opportunity to completely redesign the exhibits. In 1996, all five museum galleries closed for construction and renovation. The completely redesigned Joseph and Mary Grimshaw Egyptian Gallery opened to the public in May 1999 (fig. 5). A survey of the collections undertaken during the process of packing the objects to safeguard them during construction, combined with the installation of climate systems, allowed an entirely new range of objects to be exhibited, including objects of fragile leather, rush, papyrus, and textiles, many of which had never previously been exhibited. In its new setting, with state-of-the-art climate control systems, new lighting, and many new exhibit cases, the rich Egyptian collection of the Oriental Institute is again accessible to scholars and the public alike.

1. Letter from Rockefeller to Harper, July 12, 1889, and March 3, 1890. This and following passages quoted with permission of the Department of Special Collections, Joseph Regenstein Library, University of Chicago.

2. Rockefeller to Harper, 1937 (box 56, folder 9), Department of Special Collections, Regenstein Library.

3. Charles Breasted. *Pioneer to the Past.* New York: Charles Scribner's Sons, 1947, p. 22.

4. *Pioneer,* p. 30.

5. *Pioneer,* p. 110.

6. Papers of W. R. Harper, (box 38, folder 1:3), Department of Special Collections, Regenstein Library.

7. *The Star,* February 1896, from Breasted scrapbook in the Oriental Institute archive, p. 2.

8. J. H. Breasted, *The Oriental Institute.* Chicago: University of Chicago Press, 1933, p. 3.

9. Breasted to Hutchinson, December 4, 1919, in the Oriental Institute archive.

10. For the respective bibliographies, see Miriam Lichtheim, *Telling it Briefly: A Memoir of My Life.* Fribourg: University Press Fribourg, 1999, and *Essays in Ancient Civilization Presented to Helene J. Kantor.* Edited by A. Leonard, Jr., and B. B. Williams. Chicago: Oriental Institute, 1989.

TREASURES FROM THE COLLECTION

Early Dynastic Period and Old Kingdom

(CA. 3100–2219 B.C.)

VOTIVE PLAQUE
Early Dynastic Period, Dynasty 2,
ca. 2853–2707 B.C.
Faience
H: 5 ⅛; W: 3 ¾; D: ⅝ in
(13 x 9.5 x 1.6 cm)
OIM 7911

THE CLASSIC REPRESENTATION of the human form developed very early in Egyptian history, as indicated by this faience plaque that dates to the Early Dynastic Period (ca. 2730 B.C.). The man is shown holding a staff—a sign of rank—in his left hand. His left foot is advanced as if stepping forward. He wears a short false beard and a kilt wrapped around his waist, its belt knotted at his navel. He stands upon an artificial base line and he faces to the right—the dominant orientation of figures in Egyptian art. All of these features remained a part of the standard representation of humans well into the Roman era nearly 3,000 years later.

This plaque, along with a group of approximately 160 faience figures of animals (mainly baboons, the representation of the god Hedj-wer), thirty ivory carvings, and beads, were recovered from a pit beneath the temple of the god Khenti-amenti at Abydos. It is assumed that the objects were cleared out of the temple after they were no longer needed. The date of the deposition of the materials is unclear. William Flinders Petrie, who excavated the deposit, dated it to the middle of Dynasty 2, while more recent work by Barry Kemp suggests a much wider range of dates from the end of the Old Kingdom to early Dynasty 18. Although the objects in the cache may date to various periods within that time span, the style of this plaque strongly argues for an Early Dynastic date of manufacture.

The earliest examples of figurative art in relief appear on decorated mace heads, palettes, and on the stelae that marked ceremonial burials at Abydos. This plaque is from a temple context, hence it is an early—and rare—example of a votive object commissioned by an individual to record his image, name, and titles to accrue favor from the gods. The practice of placing non-funerary plaques or stelae in temples by private devotees was strongly associated with Abydos. By the Middle Kingdom, kings and private individuals alike constructed shrines to house commemorative stelae that allowed them to symbolically partake of the festivals of renewal associated with the rituals of the god Osiris (see no. 15).

Only a tentative translation of the brief inscription can be suggested. Alternate readings of the personal name and title are possible, and the geographic name Hemen (also read Mehen or Mensk) is otherwise unattested.

Inscription:
Supervisor of Festivals (?), Netcherti of Hemen(?).

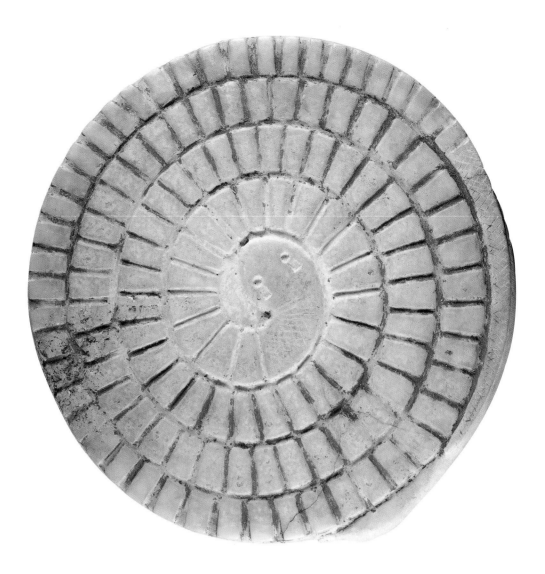

2.

MEHEN GAME BOARD

Old Kingdom, Dynasties 3–6,
ca. 2707–2219 B.C.
Egyptian alabaster (calcite)
D: 14 ³/₄; H: 1 ³/₄ in (38 x 4.5 cm)
OIM 16950

THE ANCIENT EGYPTIANS enjoyed a wide variety of board games. One game in the form of a coiled serpent is named Mehen after a serpent deity who was thought to protect the sun god during his passage through the dark hours of the night. Texts indicate that Mehen imprisoned the enemies of the sun god within its coils, while other representations show Mehen protectively encircling the sun god. The objective of the Mehen game was to travel along the coils of the snake's body to reach the area where, symbolically, the sun god dwelled, and hence, to join that god in his cycle of eternal rebirth. Two or four opponents started play at the tail, which, for unknown reasons, is in the form of a duck's head. They moved the game pieces, in the forms of small lions and round marbles, along the squares of the serpent's coils.

There is considerable variety in Mehen games. Some have nearly 400 squares, while this example has only 127, and the snake may be coiled in a clockwise or counterclockwise direction. Mehen games have been recovered from Predynastic and Old Kingdom sites. Although the game apparently fell out of favor after the Old Kingdom, it is again depicted in scenes in Dynasty 26 (664 B.C.) tombs, the decoration of which often incorporated entire scenes from much earlier monuments.

3.

PANEL FROM THE TOMB OF NEFERMAAT AND ITET

Old Kingdom, late Dynasty 3–early Dynasty 4, reigns of Huni and Snefru, ca. 2639 B.C.

Limestone, colored paste

H: 118; W: 36 ¼; D: 3 ½ in (299.72 x 92.7 x 8.89 cm)

OIM 9002

THIS STONE PANEL COMES from the north doorjamb of the west wall of the facade of the tomb chapel of Itet at Medum. Itet was the wife of prince Nefermaat, who was probably the eldest son of King Huni. Nefermaat's half brother, King Snefru, built two great pyramids at Dahshur, and at least finished, if not entirely built, the pyramid at Medum. Itet and her husband were buried in a double mastaba equipped with two stone-lined chapels, one for him, the other for her. Although this section of the decoration came from her tomb chapel, conventions of Egyptian art and rules of decorum, which gave the husband primacy of place over his wife, dictated that Nefermaat be more prominently shown. He is standing in the top register, while the smaller figure of Itet is shown in the middle register. The couple's two sons stand behind their mother. Four other sons, or grandsons, are shown in the lowest register.

Like other sections of the tomb, this piece is remarkable for its technique. Rather than being carved or painted, the limestone has been carved in rough sunk relief and the recesses filled with colored paste. The recesses were left very rough, with irregular indentations to allow the paste to adhere to the stone surface. It has been suggested that since this technique is known only from the mastaba of Nefermaat and Itet, and from an inscription on the base of a statue of their son, Hemiunu, that Nefermaat himself invented it. The inscription before Nefermaat proclaims, "He is one who made his images (literally "gods") in writing that cannot be erased." The reference to "gods" is an allusion to the potency of hieroglyphic texts—the "words of the god"—which were thought to have been given to mankind by the gods. It is unclear if the evident pride in the accomplishment is an indication that Nefermaat invented the new and attractive technique or that he took satisfaction in knowing that the tomb could not be usurped by simply recutting the inscriptions.

The huge mastaba of Nefermaat and Itet (tomb no. 16), stands to the northeast of the ruined pyramid of Huni at Medum. The stone panels with inlaid paste were widely dispersed between Cairo and other museum collections. Other sections of the tomb chapels were painted rather than inlaid. The famous painting, "the Medum geese," was recovered from the chapel of Itet.

Inscriptions:

Upper register: Nefermaat. He is one who made his images (literally: gods) in writing that cannot be erased.

Middle register: The King's Acquaintance, Itet; [Seref]-ka, Ankh-er-fened.

Lower register: Wehem-ka, Shepses-ka, Ankh-er-sheret-ef, Ka-khenet.

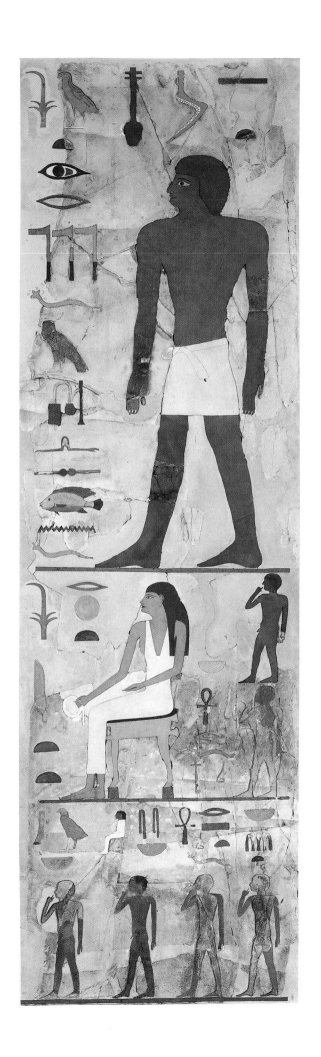

4.

FALSE DOOR OF NY-SU-REDI

Old Kingdom, late Dynasty 4,
ca. 2500 B.C.
Limestone
H: 19 ½; W: 12 ½; D: ⅓ in
(50 x 32 x 6 cm)
OIM 10825

A FALSE DOOR is an architectural element found in tombs that was thought to give the soul of the deceased access from the dark underground burial chamber to the decorated tomb chapel. False doors could be very elaborate, being composed of multiple jambs decorated with scenes and inscriptions and often, as here, with a rectangular tablet that shows the deceased seated before a table of offerings.

This false door came from the otherwise unknown tomb chapel of the Overseer of the Craftsmen, Ny-su-redi. The rectangular tablet shows him seated, stretching one arm toward the table of offerings that is heaped with stacks of tall loaves of bread. He is seated on a stool with bovine legs and a papyrus umbel, a symbol of rebirth, at the back.

The representation of the doorway opening is surrounded by a lintel and jambs inscribed with the name and titles of the deceased. The spirit of Ny-su-redi, wearing a simple wrapped kilt, is shown emerging from the door. Representations of the deceased emerging from a false door show many variations in the Old Kingdom. Some are done in low raised or sunk relief, while other false doors have complete statues, which seem to be stepping from the burial shaft.

The cursory way in which Ny-su-redi's names are written toward the bottom of each outer jamb is curious. Since the representation of the deceased and the other inscriptions end roughly on the same level, it appears that the names were added to the jambs as an afterthought. The false door may have originally been designed to be installed in conjunction with an offering slab that would have obscured the lower, then uninscribed, section. Perhaps the monument was ultimately displayed by itself, and it was thought desirable to fill in the empty spaces on each side.

Inscriptions:

Left jamb: A gift that the king gives, [namely] a burial in the western necropolis and a good old age [to] Ny-su-redi.

Right jamb: A gift that Anubis Lord of the [Sacred] Land [consisting of] invocation offerings for him of bread and beer during the festival of Thoth and the wag festival [to] Ny-su-redi.

Horizontal text and right interior jamb: The Overseer of the Craftsmen, Ny-su-redi.

Inner jamb, left: The Inspector of the Craftsmen, Ny-su-redi.

5.

**THE CONFECTIONER,
TCHENENET**

Old Kingdom, late Dynasty 4–
early Dynasty 5, ca. 2504 B.C.
Granite
H: 17 ³/₄ in (45.5 cm)
OIM 14054

THIS STATUE REPRESENTS a man stiffly seated on a stool, his feet firmly planted on the base upon which the stool is positioned. He wears a blunt-cut, shoulder-length wig without a part, the strands of which are indicated by lines scored in the granite. He wears a knee-length kilt. The belt that secures the kilt is indicated across his back by two parallel lines.

Granite, from which this statue is carved, was quarried at Aswan on the southern border of Egypt. It was favored for private statuary in Dynasty 3 through the early part of Dynasty 5, and thereafter it was largely replaced by limestone. Granite was among the most laborious stones to work, for the copper tools used by the artists were ineffective against it, and it had to be worked with pounders of harder stone such as dolorite. Ironically, granite could not be finished as finely as the more commonly used limestone, and hence granite statues tend to be coarse compared to those of softer stones (compare nos. 7, 8, and 35). Unlike limestone statues that were painted, those of granite were rarely pigmented other than for the eyes, lips, and details of clothing. The lack of pigmentation may be due to a special reverence for the mottled color of the granite. No trace of pigment is preserved on this example.

The rough texture of this granite almost obscures the brief text that appears on the left and right of the feet and which gives the name of the owner and his profession "The Confectioner, Tchenenet." It is not known in what sort of institution he worked. Statues of granite are usually restricted to people of high rank who could "afford" a luxury product, yet the title of Tchenenet does not indicate that he was of the cultural elite.

This statue was probably constructed for the tomb of Tchenenet. It was intended to preserve his likeness for eternity and to provide an abode for his spirit (*ka*) after his death. A lintel from a like-named man was discovered near Giza, suggesting that this statue may be from the same area.

Inscription:
The confectioner, Tchenenet.

6.

SINGERS AND DANCERS

Old Kingdom, Dynasty 5,
ca. 2504–2347 B.C.
Limestone
H: 14 3/8; W: 11; D: 1 15/16 in
(37 x 28 x 5 cm)
OIM 10590

SCENES OF SINGERS and dancers are not uncommon in Old Kingdom tombs. This fragment from an unidentified tomb shows two women and the hands of a third figure to the far left. The women on the left clap their hands to keep time to the music, while the woman on the right raises one hand and places the other on her hip as she dances. The women wear short, rounded hairstyles and tight-fitting dresses with wide shoulder straps and broad collar necklaces. The woman to the right also wears a sash tied at her hip. This ornament is characteristic garb for members of a group of professional musicians called *khener* who were employed by the palace, temples, and funerary estates. Scenes of these performers are known from tombs as early as Dynasty 4 (ca. 2639 B.C.) where they dance in association with funerary offering rites or funerary processions. A scene of *khener* in the tomb of Neb-kau-hor at Sakkara is captioned "beautiful dancing for your *ka* every day," indicating that the dancers would perform for the deceased eternally in the afterlife. Other scenes associate the *khener* with Hathor—a goddess associated with dancing—suggesting that the dances invoked that deity, and hence her blessings, for the deceased.

It is unclear if the fragmentary inscription above the women should be restored as the commonly encountered phrase "singing for the *khener* or "singing to . . . (whatever type of musical instrument was shown beside the women)."

7

**"SERVANT" STATUES FROM THE
TOMB OF NY-KAU-INPU**
Old Kingdom, Dynasty 5, probably
reign of Niuserre, ca. 2445–2414 B.C.
Limestone, pigment

THE ANCIENT EGYPTIANS believed that the afterlife was essentially a continuation of life on earth and that the soul of the deceased had the same material requirements in death as in life. They also believed that food and the pleasurable activities of daily life could be guaranteed in the afterlife by representing them in the tomb. Therefore, tomb chapels were decorated with carved and painted scenes, and some were equipped with models of goods and activities that the deceased wished to possess for eternity.

These statues are part of a group of twenty-five figures from the tomb of a cemetery official named Ny-kau-inpu. These figurines, the largest known group preserved from a single tomb, include the tomb owner and his wife, his sons and daughters, members of his household staff, and a model of a granary (see below). The standard offerings made to the deceased were bread, beer, oxen, and fowl— the same things that the statuettes are shown preparing. Other figures are shown making music, while the function of yet others (the statuettes showing leapfrog or spanking, and the dwarf with a bundle over his shoulder) is unclear. Unlike most such statuettes, several of the figures are identified as family members by brief hieroglyphic texts.

These stone statuettes evolved into wood models typical of the late Old Kingdom and Middle Kingdom (see no. 13). These were then replaced by ushebtis of the Second Intermediate Period and later. Although the theological basis of the figurines changed over time, they all shared the function of providing service to the deceased in the afterlife.

Statues from the tomb of Ny-kau-inpu, showing family members and musicians (top row) and the production of bread, food offerings, pottery, and miscellaneous themes (middle and bottom rows).

Ny-kau-inpu and His Wife, Hemet-ra-djet

H: 20 1/5; W: 13 1/2; D: 9 3/4 in
(52.4 x 34.7 x 25.3 cm)
OIM 10618

THE HIEROGLYPHIC TEXT on the base of this statue indicates that it represents the tomb owner Ny-kau-inpu and his wife Hemet-ra-djet. The woman places her arm affectionately around her husband's shoulder. Her other arm, of exaggerated length, is stiffly at her side, the fingers extended. She wears a blunt-cut wig of curls or braids, and her own hair is visible at the hairline. Her face is broad and dominated by her large and heavy nose; her eyes are placed high on her face. Her tight, heavily pleated dress with wide shoulder straps emphasizes the roundness of her belly and thighs. Her skin is painted a light yellow.

Her husband wears a traditional Old Kingdom wrapped kilt with an inverted pleat on the front. The loop of the knot that secures the kilt is visible at his waistline. He wears a rounded wig. The proportions of his body are highly abstracted; the distance from his foot to knee is very short while the length from his knee to his waist is overly long. His limbs (as well as the arms of his wife), are strangely flattened and detailed with the indication of muscles and tendons. Each hand grasps a rounded cylinder which may be an abbreviated staff or simply the indication of negative space, although that area was not painted black as was the area between the man's legs and between his toes. The figures are attached to a thick rectangular back pillar. The woman stands away from the background, leaving considerable stone between her and the support. Unlike the majority of Old Kingdom statues, here the woman stands to her husband's right.

Woman Mashing Beer

H: 11 7/8; W: 4 1/2; D: 8 1/4 in
(30.5 x 11.7 x 21.2 cm)
OIM 10635

HERE A WOMAN, identified as a daughter of Ny-kau-inpu, pushes a round sieve into a vat of beer as she strains the fermented bread from the liquid. The large vat is steadied by four supports, made of perhaps rocks or mud. The woman wears a simple wrapped kilt which reaches her mid-chest, leaving her breasts bare. A fabric cap covers much of her hair. The sculptor has managed to express the movement of the woman by portraying her left arm straight, as she supports herself on the edge of the vat. Her right shoulder is lower, her arm bent as she scoops from the vessel. The bend of the knees and the angle of her back further emphasize the effort expended in her activity.

Two Harpists

Male Dwarf Harpist
H: 4 ³/₄; W: 2 ³/₄; D: 3 ³/₄ in
(12.5 x 7.2 x 9.6 cm)
OIM 10641

Female Harpist
H: 8 ¹/₈; W: 4 ³/₈; D: 6 ¹/₄ in
(20.7 x 11 x 16.1 cm)
OIM 10642

AMONG THE MOST CHARMING of the Ny-kau-inpu statuettes are three harpists, two of which are pictured here. They lean large shovel-shaped floor harps upon their left shoulders and pluck the strings with their right hands. The upper section of each harp neck has been broken away. The left ear of the male harpist is folded out by the pressure of the harp. They wear similar garments (indicated in paint or by carving) with a single broad strap that crosses the left shoulder and leaves the right shoulder bare. The woman's hair (or wig) is blunt-cut, the curls or braids indicated by crosshatching. She sits with her knees bent, her left leg under her, the foot turned upward as it emerges from under her right ankle. Her skin is painted the same medium yellow tone as that of the third male harpist of the Ny-kau-inpu group (not pictured).

The dwarf's short legs are stretched out on either side of his harp. His hair is closely cut and his hairline is indicated in relief. Dwarfs were not uncommonly depicted in ancient Egyptian art, and there are references to dwarfs in the court where they served and amused the king.

POTTER

H: 5 ¼; W: 2 ⅝; D: 4 ¾ in
(13.2 x 6.7 x 12.5 cm)
OIM 10628

THERE ARE MANY two dimensional scenes of potters at work; however, this statue is a unique example of this genre in the round. The potter crouches before a potter's wheel which, in this period, is in the form of a low turntable. He turns the platform with his left hand while his right hand forms the rim of the vessel. The arduousness of the potter's profession is indicated by the way the ribs (represented as parallel lines) stand out on the man's arched back, the thinness of his legs, and the prominence of his collarbones. He is thin, and his hairline has heavily receded, suggesting a long life of hard work such as that described in the ancient text *The Satire on the Trades*: "He [the potter] grubs in the mud more than a pig, in order to fire his pots; His clothes are stiff with clay; He makes a pounding with his feet, and he himself is crushed. He grubs the yard of every house and roams the public places."

8.

**NEN-KHEFET-KA AND HIS WIFE
NEFER-SHEMES**

Old Kingdom, Dynasty 5,
reigns of Menkauhor and Unis,
ca. 2414-2347 B.C.
Limestone, pigment
H: 27 in (69.3 cm); Base: H: 13 ¼;
W: 11 ¾; D: ⅞ in (34 x 30 x 2.3 cm)
OIM 2036 A-B

THIS STATUE OF NEN-KHEFET-KA being embraced by his wife Nefer-shemes incorporates the essential elements of Old Kingdom funerary statues: the representation of the deceased in imperishable stone and the individual's names and titles. Nen-khefet-ka wears a knee-length kilt with a starched inverted pleat. The fabric belt is knotted near his navel. His wig is in the heavy curled style favored during this period. The area within his clenched fists is sculpted to perhaps represent empty space, for to actually hollow out the hands would have left them vulnerable to damage.

As was typical of Old Kingdom statuary, the flesh of the male is painted a reddish-orange while the woman is a pale yellow, perhaps an allusion to the more sheltered female who did not work outside in the sun. Nefer-shemes wears a tightly fitted white, v-neck gown and a green choker. Her own hair is visible on her forehead emerging from beneath her heavy blunt-cut wig.

The statue is socketed into a separate slightly trapezoidal base, which is incised with the name and titles of the deceased.

In 1897, when Flinders Petrie excavated the statue chamber (*serdab*) of the ruined mastaba of Nen-khefet-ka at Deshasheh, he found fragments of at least twelve statues, all of which, including this example, had been deliberately smashed in antiquity. This damage may have been inflicted upon the figures by an enemy of the tomb owner in an attempt to "kill" him in the afterlife. Other statues of Nen-khefet-ka are in the Museum of Fine Arts Boston, the Museum of Archaeology and Anthropology at the University of Pennsylvania, The British Museum, and the Egyptian Museum, Cairo.

The press, clearly infected by the enthusiasm of James Henry Breasted, announced the 1897 arrival of this statue in Chicago thus: "In September, Nen Khefetka and his wife, millionaire nobles who flourished on the banks of the Nile about three thousand years before the birth of Christ, will hold a formal reception at the Haskell Museum for the faculty of the board of trustees and 'friends of the university.'"

Inscription:

Overseer of Commissions, King's Acquaintance, Chief of the Southern Goat City, Royal Priest, King's Acquaintance, Nen-khefet-ka.

9.

LINTEL OF KHA-BAU-PTAH

Old Kingdom, Dynasty 5, reign of
Niuserre or later, ca. 2445–2414 B.C.

Limestone

L: 29 ¼; W: 12 ³/₈; D: 1 ½ in

(75 x 32 x 4 cm)

OIM 10815

KHA-BAU-PTAH WAS AN OFFICIAL who served as a priest of the funerary cults of the Dynasty 5 kings Sahure, Neferirkare, and Niuserre, as well as being a priest of Re and Hathor in the Sun Temple of Neferirkare. This left hand section of a lintel from his tomb at Sakkara indicates that he also served as the "Overseer of Royal Manicurists." The false door from that tomb also records the title "Overseer of the Royal Hairdressers." The combination of such positions is a reminder that many priestly positions were part-time, allowing the priest to pursue a variety of occupations.

On this lintel, Kha-bau-ptah sits on a stool whose bovine-shaped legs rest on drums. He holds a scepter in his right hand, a staff of rank in his left. Details of his dress may have been added in paint which is now eroded. The tomb was discovered by Auguste Mariette in 1877.

Inscription:

The one revered by the great god, [revered] by the king, beloved of his lord, the Overseer of the Royal Manicurists, Kha-bau-ptah.

10.

A WARNING TO TOMB ROBBERS

Old Kingdom, late Dynasty 6,
ca. 2219 B.C.

Limestone

H: 18 ¹/₄; W: 16 ⁵/₈; D: 1 ⁵/₈ in
(46.6 x 42.7 x 4 cm)

OIM 10814

THIS RELIEF WAS PART OF the decoration of the tomb chapel of the courtier Biw which was located northeast of the pyramid of the Dynasty 6 King Pepi II at Sakkara. Biw, who bore the titles "Lector Priest" and "Sole Companion of the King," wears a broad collar necklace, a short goatee, and holds a staff, a symbol of his rank. The fragment of the text above his head can be reconstructed from other similar texts as a warning that "Anyone who enters this tomb unlawfully, I will seize him like a bird." Tomb chapels, with their decorated walls, were open to those who wished to say a prayer on behalf of the deceased, and this type of text is a vivid reminder that even in the Old Kingdom, vandals were of concern to the tomb owner.

The fragment is carved in sunk relief in a flat, unornamented style with little detail added to the interior of the hieroglyphs. Biw's eye, indicated by a simple oval, is greatly out of scale to his face, and his arms are depicted as dropping stiffly from his broad shoulders. These stylistic features, which are characteristic of the late Old Kingdom, were imitated by artists of Dynasty 26, some 1,500 years later.

Inscription:
Biw, he says. . . this tomb. . . a bird. . . necropolis. The Sole Companion, Biw.

11.

THE ROYAL HERALD, NENI
Old Kingdom, Dynasty 6,
ca. 2347–2216 B.C.
Wood, gesso, paint, red ochre
H: 25 1/3 (65 cm); Base: W: 6 3/4;
D: 15; H: 1 5/8 in (17.1 x 38.1 x 4 cm)
OIM 11489

THIS STATUE OF A MAN named Neni was discovered in the statue chamber (*serdab*) of his tomb at Sedment in Middle Egypt. The statue was intended to serve as the abode for the soul of the deceased and to receive offerings that were left in the tomb.

Neni is shown with his left foot advanced. He is slender, and his head is greatly oversized for his body, making him appear almost juvenile. It is rare to see a figure this large carved of a single piece of wood. The statue has been set into a separate rectangular base that is inscribed with three lines of hieroglyphic text arranged perpendicular to the statue.

Neni is depicted wearing the classic late Old Kingdom-First Intermediate mid-calf length kilt with a stiff triangular pleat in the front. Wooden statues of courtiers of the Old Kingdom commonly either hold a staff in their left hand and a scepter (or the indication of a truncated scepter) in their right, to indicate their presumed rank, or they stand with their hands stiffly at their sides. The pose shown here, in which the individual grasps the edge of his garment with his right hand, is known from other examples from the late Old Kingdom and the Middle Kingdom. Traces of dark reddish brown pigment over areas of skin indicate that the statue was originally tinted in the color traditionally associated with males.

Inscription:

The Sole Companion of the King, the Royal Herald, the Staff Bearer, the Support of Ken-mut, Neni. A gift which the king gives to Anubis who is upon his mountain, that he may give offerings to the revered one Neni, the revered one who is revered by the great god, Neni.

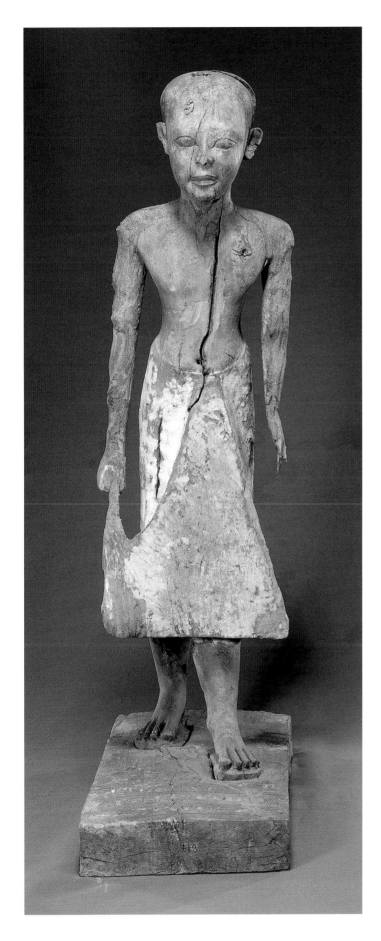

First Intermediate Period and Middle Kingdom

(CA. 2219–1550 B.C.)

12.
UHA AND HIS WIFE HENUT-SEN
First Intermediate Period,
Dynasties 7–11, ca. 2219–1995 B.C.
Limestone, pigment
H: 43 ½; W: 27 ¾ in (111.7 x 71.1 cm)
OIM 16956

FUNERARY STELAE WERE ERECTED in private tomb chapels to commemorate the name, career, and exemplary behavior of the deceased for eternity. As visitors to the tomb chapel read and recited the inscriptions incised upon the stelae, the memory of the deceased was evoked among the living. As related in the tomb of Pet-osiris some 1,500 years later, "a man is revived when his name is pronounced."

Uha, who bore the titles "Seal Bearer of the King" and "Lector Priest," is shown with his wife Henut-sen. The monument was commissioned by, and for, Uha, hence his wife as a subsidiary figure was shown on a much smaller scale. It was customary for married couples to be shown embracing and the artist cleverly solved the problem of the inequities of height by having Henut-sen place her arm around her husband's wrist rather than, as was customary, around his shoulder. Uha wears the traditional wrapped skirt with looped knot at the waist, a broad collar necklace, bracelets, and a heavily curled wig. He holds a long staff and a scepter, both of which were common symbols of authority for mid-rank officials.

Art of the First Intermediate Period more freely mixed images of completely different scales within a single scene. Here, men of diminutive scale make offerings to Uha. The man closest to him pours a beverage into a round-bottom drinking bowl in front of his mouth while the others behind and slightly below offer a haunch of beef, a gazelle, and a bird. An offering table with five small pots, three larger liquid offering vessels, and two large baskets appear near Uha's left arm. The bright and varied colors employed in this *stela*, the wide shoulders of Uha, and his long, thin, arms are all characteristic of art of the First Intermediate Period.

The texts include a conventional prayer that called upon anyone who came into the tomb chapel to admire the reliefs and to utter an invocation on behalf of the deceased. The long horizontal text contains the basic precepts of Egyptian morality: hard work, geniality, loyalty to one's family, and advancement upon one's own merit. It also contains an apparent reference to Uha's circumcision "along with 120 men." Although there is no evidence for rituals of mass circumcision, the following phrase "there was none whom I struck, and none who struck me, there was none whom I scratched and none who scratched me," does suggest such a ritual. The few sources that we have on male circumcision suggest that it took place when the boy was pre-adolescent, but certainly not an infant. Why Uha would mention it so prominently on his stela is not known.

Inscriptions:

Horizontal registers: An offering which the king gives to Anubis who is Upon his Mountain, Who is in the Wrapping, Lord of the Sacred Land [that he may give] funerary offerings consisting of bread and beer, to the count, the seal bearer of Lower Egypt, the Sole Companion, the Lector Priest, the One revered by the Great God, Lord of Heaven, Uha, justified. He says: "I was one beloved of his father, praised by his mother, one whom his brothers and sisters love. When I was circumcised along with 120 men, there was none whom I struck, and none who struck me, there was none whom I scratched and none who scratched me. I was an excellent citizen who lived by his [own] possessions, who ploughed with his [own] team of oxen, who sailed in his [own] boat, not with what I received from the hand of my father Uha (senior).

Vertical text: Oh living ones upon earth, you shall say, "A thousand of bread, beer, oxen, and fowl, and a thousand of every good thing for the revered one, the count, Uha."

Above Henut-sen: His wife, the Sole Royal Ornament, Priestess of Hathor, the revered one, Henut-sen.

13.

MODEL WORKSHOP

First Intermediate Period,
Dynasties 9–10, ca. 2170–2025 B.C.
Wood, gesso, pigment, linen
W: 14; D: 8; H: 4 ½ in
(36 x 23 x 11.5 cm)
OIM 11495

MODELS OF WORKSHOPS were placed in tombs, for it was believed that the tiny figures of the model could eternally provide the services or goods portrayed for the deceased in the afterlife. Wooden workshop models, staffed by many workers, are characteristic of the Middle Kingdom. They are derived from simpler Old Kingdom statues of workers which were either singly, or in groups, deposited in tombs (see no. 7). The Middle Kingdom versions were less expensive and easier to manufacture than the earlier stone examples. This model was excavated by Petrie and Brunton at Sedmet El Gebel (the necropolis of Herakleopolis), where it was discovered in a statue niche (*serdab*) cut into the east wall of a tomb's burial chamber.

This model workshop combines the industries of baking, brewing, and slaughtering, which produced the components for the standard funerary offerings of bread, beer, and oxen. These fundamental needs were thereby met by one economical model.

Baking and brewing were closely associated, for beer was made from bread mash. The first step in the process is represented by a woman bent over a hand mill, grinding grain into flour (shown in the lower left-hand corner). Another woman seated near the mill assists, collecting the flour into a basket (now lost). The rectangular striped object may be an inverted basket. The stout cylinder with a jar on top is a brazier, perhaps for cooking the mash. Five beer jars with dark mud stoppers sit in a basket. Two larger white jars separate this scene from that of the slaughter. The two round vats at the cow's back are difficult to interpret. The geometric markings on the top of the one attended by the man suggest that he may be engaged in sieving the beer mash (see no. 7). Most of the figures employed in bread and beer production are, as indicated by the lighter tone of their skin, women, while the butchers, with their darker reddish skin, are men.

A trussed cow, with its neck upturned, lies amongst the butchers. Its tail, which is curled up over its flank, is indicated in paint. A man with a knife stands above the cow's neck while another man collects blood that spurts from the severed neck. A similar model from the tomb of Meketre suggests that the cylinder at the cow's back is a pot of blood which was collected to make blood pudding. The man holding a fan with which to fan the fire is a common element in cooking scenes. His presence suggests that the vat of blood at the corner of the model is supposed to be above a brazier used to cook the pudding.

As is typical of models of the First Intermediate Period, the workers are highly abstracted stick figures with peg-like limbs. The artist seems to have had only two alternatives for producing the figures—either standing or sitting. Therefore, the workers who are supposed to bend over the vats or the cow are simply standing figures who lean rather than bend. The faces are very rudimentary with beak-like noses. The hair of the male and female workers is nearly the same. The eyes are indicated in paint and each figure is wrapped in a small piece of linen to suggest clothing.

14.

A LETTER TO THE DEAD

First Intermediate Period,
Dynasty 11, ca. 2119–1976 B.C.
Baked clay, pigment
H: 8 7/8 (23 cm); D (top): 3 1/2 in (9 cm)
OIM 13945

THE ANCIENT EGYPTIANS believed that the barrier between the worlds of the living and the dead was permeable and that people could communicate with the deceased by various means including the written word. Such written communications, called Letters to the Dead, are first attested in the Old Kingdom (ca. 2500 B.C.). The letters, usually an appeal for help from a deceased relative, were written on papyrus, linen, or pottery figurines, but most commonly on clay bowls into which offerings may have been placed to attract the spirit of the deceased. The letters were most probably left in the tomb chapel, where the spirit would easily find them.

Many of the letters begin with a summary of the individual's situation, giving the impression that it is a reminder of a previous communication, perhaps a prayer said earlier. The letters often include a promise that the petitioner will give the deceased a reward, such as food offerings, in return for his or her assistance. Many of the letters refer to individuals—living or dead—whom the writer thinks are responsible for the problems the writer faces, and contain a plea for the deceased to litigate against them from the beyond.

This letter is written on a pottery jar stand in eight vertical columns in flowing hieratic (cursive hieroglyphic) script. The letter is from an unidentified man to his deceased father, asking him to assist in the birth of a son to his wife Seny. In the

letter the man requests his father to act against two female servants whom the man blames for his wife's inability to bear a son. A supplementary line was added with the comment: "Moreover, I beg a second healthy male child for your daughter."

Inscription:

This is a reminder of what I said to you: You know that Idu said about his son, "As for whatever may be there, I will not allow him to be harmed by any affliction." Do the same for me. Indeed, now this vessel is brought [to you] in order that your mother can make litigation. It is agreeable that you should support her. Let a healthy male child be born to me. You are an excellent spirit. Indeed, as for those two, the servants who have caused Seny to be afflicted (named) Nefert-chent and Itjai, destroy them and destroy every affliction that is against my wife, for you know that I want it. Destroy it completely! As you live for me, the Great One will praise you, and the face of the great god will be glad over you. He will give you pure bread with his two hands. Moreover, I beg a second healthy male child for your daughter.

15.

**STELA OF THE HOUSEHOLD
OF SENBU**

Middle Kingdom, late Dynasty 12,
early Dynasty 13, ca. 1794–1648 B.C.
Limestone
H: 18 ³/₄; W: 11 ³/₄; D: 3 ¹/₂ in
(48 × 30 × 9 cm)
OIM 6739

STELAE LIKE THIS ONE were erected by individuals, or by entire households, in commemorative chapels in northern Abydos, a site that had special sanctity because of its association with funerary deities. The chapels, some of which were associated with burials, were located along the route for the annual procession for religious festivals of Osiris. The act of placing a stela with an image of oneself in such a chapel was thought to enable the devotee to participate symbolically in the festivals of renewal enacted for the god, and also to benefit from the offerings that were left for the deity.

This monument calls upon Wepwawet, another deity of the necropolis at Abydos, who is shown twice at the top of the stela as a recumbent jackal, to grant funerary offerings in the afterlife. The uppermost register shows a man named Senbu seated before a table of funerary offerings. His wife, Sat-sobek, is seated on the ground opposite him with a small table of offerings before her. The lower registers are divided into six boxes in which other members of Senbu's household are shown. Below Senbu are two "Mistresses of the House" who have no defined relationship to Senbu, and to the right, two half-sisters ("his sister of his mother") presumably of Senbu. The third register shows the family's baker and his wife (left), their daughter and the baker's mother (right). The lowest register portrays a female servant and her son (left), and the household's brewer and his sister (right).

The women are dressed in long tight-fitting dresses. Nine of the ten wear long hair (or wigs) whose tresses fall over the shoulder. The female servant wears her hair in a high ponytail, a style associated with servant girls. The men hold a folded handkerchief, while the women touch their hands to their chest in a sign of devotion to the god.

Stelae that show households, or groups of palace personnel, are not uncommon in the late Middle Kingdom. It cannot always be determined whether such a stela was commissioned by the most prestigious person—here Senbu—or if it was made by the household staff who included their employer as a mark of respect. The fact that five of the six lower sections of the stela are given over to servants and their families, and that they are shown essentially in the same dress, position and size as Senbu and his family, suggests that the staff may have commissioned this example. The figures on many better-preserved examples of this type of stela were originally painted in blue or green pigment which would have helped distinguish the very low sunk relief carving.

Inscriptions:

Top register: A gift that the king gives to Wepwawet, Lord of the Sacred Land (i.e., the necropolis) that he may give invocation offerings consisting of bead, beer, oxen, and fowl, clothing, alabaster, and incense to the spirit of the Overseer of the Phyle, Senbu, justified. His beloved wife, Mistress of the House, Sat-sobek, justified.

2nd register: the Mistress of the House Ren-(es)-seneb, possessor of veneration; the Mistress of the House Senebu-Res his sister of his mother (his half-sister) Ren-ef-res; his sister of his mother (half-sister) Nakhti.

3rd register: The baker Ren-ef-seneb; his beloved wife, the Mistress of the House, Dedi, his daughter Sat- Inher; his mother Hetep-ni.

4th register: Her [Ren-es-res'] son Nefu-en-senebu; the servant Ren-es-res; the brewer Sa-ankhi; his sister Dedu-inher.

New Kingdom and Third Intermediate Period

(CA. 1550–664 B.C.)

16.

NAKHT AND SETH-ANTEWY

New Kingdom, Dynasty 18, reigns of
Amunhotep I to Amunhotep II,
ca. 1526–1400 B.C.

Limestone

H: 11 3/4; W: 8 7/8; D: 2 3/4 in

(30.2 x 22.7 x 7 cm)

OIM 10510

THIS STELA SHOWS THE SCRIBE of the tax assessors, Nakht, making offerings to a deity shown with a curved snout and erect ears, a form usually associated with the god Seth. The god wears a short kilt and he holds an ankh, the hieroglyph for "life" and a tall, slender, *was* scepter, the symbol for "dominion." The tail of a bull (see no. 24), a symbol of virility and power, is shown in front of his legs. Nakht wears layered skirts and a short-sleeved tunic that ties at the neck. His wig, or hair, is worn in a short rounded style. He stands behind a table heaped with loaves, vegetables, and the head of a cow. He pours a liquid offering from a round bottom vessel into a basin, and he elevates a stand with a burnt offering of a fowl and a round bread loaf. A small flame emerges from the offering stand.

The text on the stela identifies the god in two different ways. The inscription in front of the god refers to him as Antewy, a combined form of Horus and Seth, while the horizontal text below the offering scene calls him Seth. This dual identity is a reflection of the belief that a god could have more than one nature—and that he or she could have the attributes of several deities in order to express the extended power of the god.

The Egyptians viewed Seth with a certain ambivalence on account of his legendary murder of his brother Osiris. Seth was revered in his role of the enemy of the evil god Apophis, and in the New Kingdom Underworld books, as on this stela, he was combined with Horus as the "Two Gods" (i.e., Horus and Seth), or "He of the Two Faces." Theophoric names such as "Seti," which were popular in Dynasties 18 through 20, also indicate the cult of Seth was again viewed favorably.

The lunette of the stela is decorated with a hybrid composition. Rather than the more commonly seen winged disk of Behdeti, the god of Edfu (see no. 43), or double eyes, here a winged disk with a single wing appears alongside a single eye. In such compositions, the winged disk appears over the deity, or the superior member of the composition, and the eye over the officiate. The parallelism is thought to combine the protection inherent in the eye of Horus with that of the ancient winged sun disk of Behdeti.

Inscriptions:

Upper section: Making offerings of every thing, making liquid and incense offerings to this noble god—may you content yourself with everything that you desire—by the Scribe of the Tax Assessors, Nakht.

Lower section: A gift that the king gives to Seth, Lord of Tjebu (modern Qaw el Kebir) and to Mut, Mistress of Megeb (a site near Qaw el Kebir), that they may give life, prosperity, health, alertness, praise, love, and being on earth in their following, to the spirit of the Scribe of the Tax Assessors, a truly excellent man, whose character everyone knows; Nakht, of the estate of Mut.

17.
FUNERARY FIGURE OF KENAMUN

New Kingdom, Dynasty 18, reign of
Amunhotep II, ca. 1428–1400 B.C.
Wood, pigment
H: 14 ½; W: 4 ½ in (37 x 11 cm)
OIM 25648

THIS FUNERARY STATUETTE inscribed for Kenamun is from a cache of figures buried near Abu Ghurob. Although it resembles a mummiform ushebti (servant statue), the inscription, and the fact that the statue was not from a tomb, indicate that it was made to commemorate the memory of Kenamun rather than to serve as a servant in the afterlife.

Kenamun, who held the title "Hereditary Prince and Count and Overseer of Cattle" was closely associated with the royal court. His mother served as nurse to the future Amunhotep II, and thus we assume that Kenamun grew up in the royal household. His relatively modest titles belie his real influence and wealth. His beautifully decorated tomb (Theban tomb 93) in western Thebes was decorated by the best-trained workmen, and the inscriptions on the statuettes indicate that they were made in the royal workshop.

Several deposits of Kenamun funerary figurines have been discovered. The largest group, to which this figure probably belonged, was discovered by illicit diggers in 1915, and an additional group of approximately seventy figures was discovered at the same site during government excavations in 1919. The later excavation was motivated by illicit digging that was interrupted. As a government agent recorded: "On the evening of the 7th of September 1919 . . . the gaffir (guardian) Mohamed Bahur was making his usual round; while at a distance of some 20 or 30 metres from the threatened spot, he saw six persons digging. Before he could recognize them, they began firing on him with revolvers—fortunately he was not touched. Finding himself in danger, he took cover behind a donkey standing there and fired in return . . ."

A third cache of Kenamun figures from Abydos contained another funerary statue (OIM 18210) that was buried near a figure of the king (OIM 5657), again an indication of the king's favor to Kenamun.

Inscription:
Made as a favor of the king for the Hereditary Prince and Count, Overseer of the Cattle of Amun, Kenamun.

18.
CHILD'S TUNIC
New Kingdom, Dynasty 18,
ca. 1473 B.C.
Linen
L: 37 5/8; W: 28 3/8 in (97 x 73 cm)
OIM 18285

THIS SIMPLE GARMENT is made of a length of almost diaphanous linen. The finely woven fabric has selvages on both sides. It has been folded in half and the sides seamed from the hem upward, leaving a ten-and-a-quarter inch arm opening to serve as a slightly capped sleeve. The bottom hem is rolled, and the hem is whipped. The key-hole shaped neck opening was cut out of the fabric and the rough edges carefully turned and stitched. The short length and the small neck opening (seven-and-a-half inches in length and five inches wide) suggest that it was made for a child. The base of the neck opening is ripped as if someone, in antiquity, tore the neck trying to fit it over his or her head.

This garment points out difficulties in interpreting Egyptian art. Most representations of clothing (see nos. 7, 8) show elaborate form-fitting dresses while most actual examples of Egyptian clothing are simple, sack-like garments similar to this one. Most depictions of children show them naked or dressed in a simple belt. This discrepancy between the artistic and archaeological record may be due to the artists' desire to emphasize the sensuality of the human body—a reflection of fertility as a focus of religious beliefs.

This tunic was one of three similar garments discovered among mummy wrappings in an anonymous burial at Gourna. That burial was covered by debris from the construction of the tomb of Senenmut (Theban Tomb 353), indicating that the burial, and hence the tunics, must be earlier than the building of Senenmut's tomb. The tunics are very similar in style to others recovered from the tomb of Ramose and Hat-nofer, the parents of Senenmut.

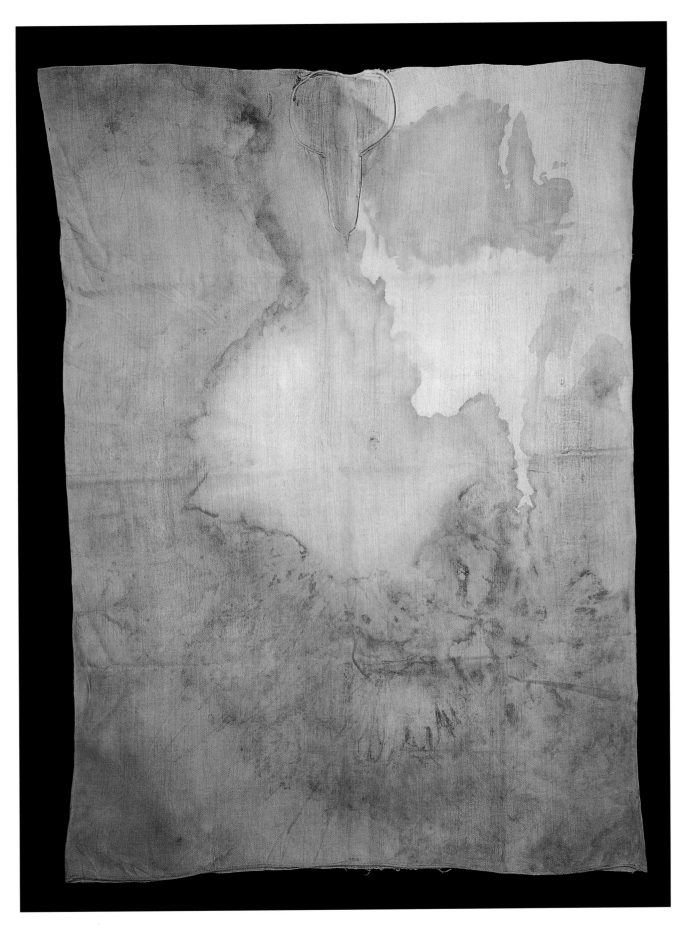

19.

STATUE OF A GOD

New Kingdom, Dynasty 18, reign of
Amunhotep III, ca. 1390–1353 B.C.

Granodiorite

H: 26 1/8; W: 15 3/4; D: 10 in

(67.2 x 40.7 x 25.5 cm)

OIM 10607

THIS SLIGHTLY UNDER-LIFE-SIZE fragment of a statue represents an unidentified god. He wears a tripartite wig, the hair indicated by striations that pass directly over the crown of the head. His false beard is indicated by a braided pattern executed in high relief. He wears a broad collar necklace and carries a staff in the form of a *was*, the hieroglyphic sign for "dominion." The eyes are almond-shaped, and the upper and lower lids are marked by heavy bands that extend into a long straight cosmetic line.

The identity of the god represented by this statue cannot be determined because it lacks distinctive attributes, or an inscription, that would associate it with a particular deity. Although it has been suggested that it represents Tatenen, one of the creator gods, the statue lacks the distinctive horned crown of that deity.

The style of the statue, and the use of black granodiorite, clearly indicate that it was one in an extensive series of divine images commissioned by Amunhotep III. Hundreds of statues, the majority portraying the goddess Sekhmet, were produced in his reign. They have been recovered from the Sudan, as well as from many locations through the Egyptian Nile Valley. Most are in hard black granodiorite, the color of which may be evocative of the dark earth, and hence fertility and rejuvenation. While the place where this example originally stood is unknown, many others like it, carved from the same stone, have been found in the ruins of the mortuary temple of Amunhotep III in western Thebes.

As was common in ancient Egypt, the facial features of this statue were closely patterned upon statues of the king himself, stressing the pharaoh's divine aspect and his association with the gods.

20.

GAME OF TWENTY SQUARES

New Kingdom, Dynasties 18–19,
ca. 1550–1070 B.C.
Wood
L: 7 ½; W: 2 ⅔ in (19.3 x 7 cm)
OIM 371

THE GAME OF TWENTY SQUARES was popular throughout the ancient Near East, and examples have been recovered from Mesopotamia, Syria, Palestine, and Cyprus as well as Egypt. The earliest examples, dated to 2600 B.C., were recovered from the royal tombs at Ur in Iraq.

The game was played by two opponents, each of whom had five playing pieces. The game pieces were made in many shapes and of materials such as stone, glass, faience, and pottery. Play began with the pieces lined up on the undecorated surfaces of the board, then moved down the side squares and up the middle of the board. The first player to successfully remove all his pieces from the board won the game. Part of the strategy of the game involved creating an obstacle of two or more pieces which could not be passed by the opponent's markers. Many boards have special markings indicating hazards and advantages. This game is related, but not identical to, another game called *senet* which had three rows of ten squares. Unlike many rectangular game boards which are double-sided (one side for the game of Twenty Squares, the other for *senet*), the bottom of this example is unmarked.

The number of moves while playing was determined by throw sticks, astragali (knucklebones), or square or tetrahedral dice. Square dice appear in Egypt in the late New Kingdom (late second millennium B.C.). As with modern dice, the examples from Egypt and the ancient Near East have opposing sides whose sum equals seven.

Board games were more than simple recreation. Scenes in tombs show a single player seated before a *senet* board or game of Twenty Squares equipped with two sets of markers, yet without a visible opponent, suggesting that the unseen player is the judge of the afterlife or the forces of evil and that winning the game was allegorically linked to rebirth. This theological symbolism is further reinforced by the name "*senet*," which means "passing," hence a reference to the journey through the underworld to rebirth.

21.

**DETAIL OF A FUNERARY
PROCESSION**

New Kingdom, Dynasty 18, reigns of
Thutmose IV-Amunhotep III,
ca. 1400–1353 B.C.
Mud brick, plaster, pigment
H: 15 ½; W: 17; D: 2 ¼ in
(40 x 43.5 x 5.8 cm)
OIM 11047

THIS FRAGMENT FROM THE WALL of the tomb of Huy at Thebes once was
part of an elaborate scene of a funerary procession in which a shrine containing
the coffin of the deceased was dragged to the tomb. The section shown here portrays the oxen who were hitched by ropes to the funerary shrine, and a funerary
priest, who wears a full, rounded wig and a simple white wrapped kilt with a wide
belt. He carries a situla, a ritual vessel (see no. 50), in his left hand and a pen box
and a group of reed pens in his right hand. Originally, this priest was followed by
four men and members of the family of the deceased. This sort of composition
was very popular as a theme for tomb decoration from the Old Kingdom into the
Late Period.

While most such scenes show two oxen, the tomb of Huy shows four, a pair of red
and black oxen in each register. According to the conventions of Egyptian art, the
colors employed for the animals served to differentiate the superimposed animals,
rather than being a reflection of their actual color. A few more complete versions
of this scene, a notable example being in the tomb of Rekhmire at Thebes, also
divide the ox procession into two registers of two animals each.

The brief inscription before the priest, "purifying with milk," is a reference to the
ritual of pouring milk before a funerary cortege.

Inscriptions:
Before the priest: Purifying with milk.
Before and above oxen: Let be said to the oxen, "Pull very hard! Do not allow your hearts to become weary!"
Above lower oxen: The oxen of his funerary estate are pulling in peace.
Behind priest: The men of Pe [in reference to men behind the priest].

22.

RUNNING IBEXES

New Kingdom, mid-Dynasty 18,
ca. 1400 B.C.
Limestone
H: 28 ½; W: 11 ¾; D: 2 ⅓ in
(73 x 30 x 6 cm)
OIM 11398

THE NUBIAN IBEX (*Capra ibex nubiana*) was a popular theme for artists from the Predynastic Period onward. As early as the Old Kingdom, they were shown in funerary offering processions where they were led on leashes and hence were presumably intended as meat offerings for the deceased. Scenes of ibexes in pens further suggest they were bred for meat.

The grace of the ibex was especially admired by the Egyptians. Love poetry compared the lover, darting toward his beloved, to an ibex. Ibexes were used as decorative motives on small luxury items, such as combs, furniture, ointment vessels, and pottery. Mummified ibexes—perhaps pets—have been recovered from private tombs.

This fragment once was part of a larger tomb wall which showed a scene of the desert hunt. The wildness of the animals is emphasized by the undulating mountainous baseline, which has been substituted for the standard flat baseline. Such scenes of the hunter in pursuit of desert creatures became popular in the middle of Dynasty 18, and this freer sort of composition was especially favored by artists of the Amarna Period (reign of Akhenaten, ca. 1352–1336 B.C.). Not only did these scenes preserve an enjoyable leisure activity of the tomb owner, but they also were allegories that refer to the balance of the forces of chaos (symbolized by the wild animals) and order (the hunter). The Nubian ibex is still found in the Sinai and the Eastern Desert of Egypt.

23.

COLOSSAL STATUE OF TUTANKHAMUN

New Kingdom, Dynasty 18, reign of
Tutankhamun, ca. 1334–1325 B.C.
Red quartzite, pigment
H: 17' 3" (525.7 cm); Base: L: 48 ¾;
W: 31 ¼; H: 23 in (125 x 80 x 59 cm)
OIM 14088

TWO COLOSSAL STATUES of a post-Amarna king were excavated by the
Oriental Institute from the ruins of the broad hall of the mortuary temple of Aye
and Horemheb, located just north of the temple of Ramesses III at Medinet Habu.
Although both statues were fragmentary, their facial features were relatively intact.
The arms and legs of the Chicago statue were restored in the style of other, con-
temporary, statues, and the base was modeled after the base of the Cairo statue
(JE 59869).

The king is shown wearing the double crown above the striped *nemes* head cover
with coiled uraeus; the straight, plaited, royal false beard; a broad collar necklace;
and the *shendyt* kilt with a belt inscribed with a cartouche. A dagger with a falcon-
form pommel, stuck obliquely into the belt, is indicated in low relief. The figure
stands with left foot advanced, his arms at his sides. The hands grasp truncated
cylinders which may represent document cases (*mekes*), or symbolic scepters.

The statue exhibits many characteristics of the post-Amarna Period. The belly of
the statue is soft and slightly rounded, emphasized by the dip of the belt below the
stomach area. The youthful face has full lips, a slightly upturned nose, and small
almond eyes emphasized by heavy cosmetic lines. The back pillar, with rounded
top, is divided into two vertical lines of text, incised and painted blue with the full
titulary of Horemheb.

The base of the statue is slightly trapezoidal, indicating that the statues flanked
a doorway. The front of the base bears a rectangle enclosing two cartouches and
epithets of Horemheb. His cartouches and titulary are also incised on the sides of
the base. Remains of a pair of small feet next to the king preserved on the Cairo
base indicate that a much smaller figure of the queen originally stood alongside
her husband.

Although the names of Horemheb appear on the statue, the cartouches and many
of the epithets on the back pillar have been recut, indicating that the statue was
appropriated from an earlier ruler. Traces of the original text can be restored as
the name of Aye, the predecessor of Horemheb. However, the features of the statue suggest that it was commissioned by an even earlier king. Although there are
few representations of Aye, there are many of Tutankhamun, and the youthful features of statues of that king more closely resemble the features of the unrestored
Cairo statue. That identification suggests that the statue was commissioned by
Tutankhamun for his own mortuary temple. The statue was carved but, as indicated by the lack of traces of Tutankhamun's name under those of Aye, not yet
inscribed with his royal titulary. The statues were appropriated by Aye, inscribed
and installed on either side of the western door of the broad hall of his temple.

After Aye's brief reign, the statues were reinscribed for Horemheb, who greatly expanded the mortuary temple of his predecessor.

The references to the god Amun of Karnak on the back pillar and base may be an allusion to the visit of that god, who normally resided on the east bank, to the west bank temples during festivals such as the Beautiful Feast of the Valley.

Inscriptions:

Belt buckle: Djser-kheperu-re-setep-en-re, Beloved of Amun.

Base: King of Upper and Lower Egypt, Djser-kheperu-re-setep-en-re, Son of Re, Horemheb, beloved of Amun, beloved of Amun-Re, Lord of the Thrones of the Two Lands, foremost of Karnak, given life like Re forever. Live Horus! The strong bull, keen of counsel, King of Upper and Lower Egypt, Lord of the Two Lands, Djser-kheperu-re-setep-en-re, beloved of Amun-Re.

Back pillar: The Horus, strong bull, keen of counsel, the Two Ladies, great of wonders in Karnak, King of Upper and Lower Egypt, ruler of the Nine Bows, Lord of the Two Lands, Lord of Action, Djser-kheperu-re-setep-en-re, bodily son of Re, his beloved, possessor of diadems, ruler of happiness, possessor of strength, Horemheb, beloved of Amun . . . Golden Horus, who is satisfied with truth, who causes the Two Lands to come into being, the good god, son of Amun whom the Lord of the Gods begot and whom Mut, Mistress of Heaven, bore in order than [he] might govern that which the sun encircles, possessor of diadems, Djser-kheperu-re-setep-en-re, bodily Son of Re, his beloved, his avenger, who has appeared on his throne, Lord of the Two Lands, Horemheb beloved of Amun . . .

24.
AMUN
New Kingdom, Dynasty 18,
reigns of Tutankhamun and Aye,
ca. 1334–1321 B.C.
Indurated limestone
H: 32 ³/₄; W: 9; D: 18 in
(84 x 23 x 46 cm)
OIM 10503

THIS SCULPTURE DEPICTS a male figure seated on a blocky throne. He wears a pleated kilt with belt and a shirt with straps that pass over his shoulders. The tail of a bull, symbolizing virility and power, is visible between his legs. His jewelry consists of armlets, bracelets, and a broad collar necklace edged with teardrop shaped beads. His hands are placed on top of his thighs. The left hand grasps an ankh, the hieroglyph for "life." The figure's feet rest solidly upon the platform on which the throne is placed. The legs are heavy and the ankles thick. A broad uninscribed back pillar continues upward from the back of the throne to the break at the back of the statue's neck.

The cartouches on the front of the throne give the prenomen and nomen of King Aye. However, the irregular texture of the stone within the cartouches may indicate that the present name was inscribed over the name of another, earlier king. Comparison of this statue with other very similar examples suggests that it was commissioned by Tutankhamun and that it originally showed the king in the guise of the god Amun, wearing his characteristic flat-topped crown with tall feathers.

When this statue came to the Oriental Institute in 1919, the head had been restored to show the king wearing the blue crown and a straight false beard. In 1933, the head was removed and another complete restoration, with decidedly Amarna features, was affixed. After the statue was re-identified as Tutankhamun in the guise of Amun, the second head was removed.

Inscriptions:
Left front of throne: The good god, the Lord of the Two Lands, Kheper-kheperu-re-ir-Maat, beloved of Amun-Re.
Right front of throne: The son of Re, The God's Father, Aye, beloved of Amun-Re.

25.

SETI I AND RAMESSES II

New Kingdom, Dynasty 19, reign of
Ramesses II, ca. 1279–1212 B.C.

Limestone, pigment

H: 15 ³/₈; W: 20; D: (max) 2 ³/₄ in
(39.5 x 51.3 x 7 cm)

OIM 10507

THIS FRAGMENT OF A STELA shows King Seti I followed by his son Ramesses (later Ramesses II "The Great") (left), and two priests (right). The king wears an elaborate wig with uraeus, a broad collar necklace, and an obliquely cut skirt over a kilt ornamented with a ceremonial apron decorated with five pendent uraei. A sash is tied around the middle of his chest. He carries the crook and flail, the traditional scepters of kingship, in his left hand and a mace in his right hand. His son wears an oblique-cut kilt and his hair is arranged in a side lock distinctive of youth and of the *iwenmutef* priest who officiates in rituals celebrating his father.

The texts identify the priests as Amun-wahsu (left) and Tia (right). They are dressed in the heavy wigs and elaborate pleated garb typical of the period in which this stela was carved. Amun-wahsu pours a libation over the offering table heaped with bread and vegetables and he holds an incense burner from which smoke curls in his left hand. Tia holds a bouquet of flowers toward the king's face and raises his hand in an honorific salute.

The text above the heads of the king and the priests indicates that they are deceased, however, the name of Seti's son—his successor—is not, as would be expected, enclosed in a cartouche. A possible explanation for this is that the stela commemorates the careers of the two priests who served Seti but did not continue to officiate in the reign of his son Ramesses. If so, this stela may be interpreted as conflating two time periods. The first time period was during Amun-wahsu's life-time, when, as indicated by the texts, he served as "Scribe of the Offering Table of the Lord of the Two Lands." The name of Ramesses is not encircled by a cartouche because, at that point in Amun-wahsu's career, Ramesses was still a prince. The second time period, at which point both priests and King Seti were dead, is symbolized by their mortuary epithets, and by the act of censing and pouring a libation before the king which is typically a funerary ritual. The *ankh* sign that Ramesses holds may be a reminder of his vitality after the death of his father. The height of the king and priests relative to Ramesses may suggest that Tia, Amun-wahsu, and Seti were of the same generation. If so, the suggestion that this Tia is to be identified with "the King's True Scribe Tia," who married the sister of Ramesses II may be ruled out, for the stela suggests that the Tia shown on it died before the accession of Ramesses, which would make him far too old to have married the new king's sister.

The emphasis placed upon the action of Amun-wahsu suggests that this stela was commissioned by him for a memorial chapel, or perhaps his own tomb, to com-memorate his role in the cult of the royal family. The relationship between the two priests is not clear, but it is possible that they were brothers, under which circum-stance it would be appropriate to share a funerary monument.

Inscriptions:

Above Seti: The Osiris, the king, Lord of the Two Lands, Men-Maat-re, Seti-mery-n-ptah, repeating of life, possessor of veneration.

Above Ramesses: The bodily son of the king, his beloved, Ramesses.

Left priest: The Osiris, the Scribe of the Offering Table of the Lord of the Two Lands, Amun-wahsu, justified, repeating of life.

Right priest: The Osiris, the Royal Scribe, Tia, justified.

26.

TWO SCENES OF NATURE

New Kingdom, Dynasties 19–21,
ca. 1292–946 B.C.

Limestone, pigment

ANIMALS
H: 4 3/4; W: 8 1/3; D: 3/4 in
(21.5 x 12.2 x 2.8 cm)
OIM 16880

GRASSHOPPERS IN A BUSH
H: 6 3/4; W: 4 15/16; D: 1 1/4 in
(17.2 x 12.7 x 3.1 cm)
OIM 16879

ANCIENT EGYPTIAN ARTISTS often used flakes of fine-textured white limestone as sketch pads. On one example shown here, two grasshoppers are depicted above a bush that bears small red berries or flowers. In the upper right a bird emerges from a nest that holds three eggs. In contrast to the carefully drawn insects and foliage, the bird and nest are drawn as cursive hieroglyphs. The symbolism, if any, of the composition is unknown. Traces of registers of black, now illegible hieroglyphic text can be seen under the grasshoppers, indicating that the flake was reused.

The scene with animals is a more formalized composition. The register lines are drawn in red and a red preliminary sketch can be seen under some parts of the figures. The animals are not a unified composition but rather are in five separate groups, suggesting that the artist was experimenting with genre studies of animals to incorporate into other works.

The top register shows a group of grazing gazelles and a pack of wild boars. The artist has painted the boars alternately black and brown to differentiate each animal in the pack. The cow with her calf and crocodile eating a fish in the lower register are compositions known from Old Kingdom tomb reliefs.

27.
THE BAD BOY
New Kingdom, Dynasty 19,
ca. 1200 B.C.
Limestone, pigment
H: 3 ⅛; W: 4 ¹⁵/₁₆ in
(7.8 x 12.6 cm)
OIM 13951

Flakes of limestone (ostracon) with drawings are well attested for the late New Kingdom. Although they vary in theme and style, it is assumed that they are either satirical drawings or illustrations of popular folk tales. This example shows a mouse dressed in a finely pleated kilt, standing on a dais before a stool. He leans on a papyrus umbel-topped staff, in imitation of a high official leaning on his staff of office. To the right, a cat stands on his back feet, wielding a flower-shaped baton over a young boy whose arms are raised in supplication. The boy wears a hairstyle associated with youth: the side lock and three tufts of hair. As was customary with children, he is shown naked.

The composition may be a satirical scene that portrays the world turned upside-down. Here, the mouse is superior to the cat, and both judge the boy. The reverse of this scene bears an inscription in hieratic: "the cat and mouse bring in the boy."

The scene was painted with full attention to detail. As with formal works, a preliminary sketch executed in red pigment can be seen under the final black outline.

28.

**STELA DEDICATED TO THE GOD
RESHEP**

New Kingdom, Dynasties 19–20,
ca. 1292–1070 B.C.
Limestone
H: 9 ³/₄; W: 6 ⁵/₈ in (25 x 17 cm)
OIM 10569

BY THE END OF THE Middle Kingdom (ca. 1650 B.C.) foreigners had settled in Egypt bringing their own gods with them. Among these deities was Reshep, originally a West Semitic deity associated with warfare and the underworld who was identified with the Mesopotamian god of the underworld, Nergal. In Chronicles 7:25 he appears in the genealogies of "bands of soldiers for war." Reshep is first attested in Egypt in Dynasty 12 by foreign names compounded with the god's name, but by the reign of Amunhotep II (ca. 1428–1400 B.C.) in Dynasty 18, the god appears in royal reliefs, and the king even refers to himself as Reshep in the context of foreign campaigns. The god is also attested in Egypt by small bronze statues and a few stelae such as the one shown here. Although he was, to a certain degree, integrated into the Egyptian pantheon, he was worshipped mainly by settlers from western Asia. This stela reflects that ethnic appeal, for it is dedicated to a man named Merer, whose name is Egyptian, but whose father bore the very un-Egyptian name Sul, suggesting that Merer's family was foreign born.

The god is presented in a manner that seemed familiar to Egyptians, yet that served to differentiate him from the purely Egyptian gods. His tall crown, which resembles the white crown of Egyptian kings, is ornamented with a long fabric streamer. The cobra (uraeus) found on the forehead of the crown has been replaced by a gazelle head, similar to that found on diadems associated with Asiatic princesses in Egypt during the Middle Kingdom. The tasseled and scalloped hem of his kilt serves to distinguish him from Egyptian gods, as do the form of his spear and the rare representation of a sling looped over his uplifted arm.

Inscriptions:
Right: Reshep, who draws near [for battle], the great god. May he give to you all life and health every day.
Left: For the spirit of the *wab* priest of Horus-Khenty-Khety, lord of Athribis, Merer, son of Sul, justified.

29.

DECORATIVE TILES

New Kingdom, Dynasty 20, reign of
Ramesses III, ca. 1182–1151 B.C.
Faience, glaze

LAPWING
H: 3 ¹⁵/₁₆; W: 3 ³/₄; D: ½ in
(10.1 x 9.7 x 1.8 cm)
OIM 16721

CARTOUCHE
H: 4 ½; W: 4; D: ⁹/₁₆ in
(11.5 x 10.16 x 1.5 cm)
OIM 16672

DOORWAYS IN THE PALACE of Ramesses III at Medinet Habu were decorated with brightly glazed tiles. The tiles were not only colorful additions to the décor of the palace, but their motifs also expressed the power and authority of the king.

The tile with the bird bears a motto praising the king. This is composed of a lapwing (*Vanellus cristatus*), the hieroglyph for "Egyptian people." A basket, shown as a half circle under the bird, means "all." The star in the center of the tile is the verb to "give praise." Together, these elements spell the wish that "all the Egyptian people give praise." The object of adoration is the name of the king that appears in a cartouche to the left. This composition illustrates how hieroglyphs could be recombined and embedded into scenes. The uplifted human arms that emerge from the bird's breast are the usual determinative for the writing of the verb "to praise." Here they have been added to the lapwing to more explicitly stress the fact that it is all the *people* who adore the king.

This tile displays several complex techniques. Faience was pressed into a reverse mold to produce the raised areas (the bird, star, basket, and area around the cartouche). The hieroglyphs, the colored detail in the basket, and the blue of the background surrounding the bird are inlays of bits of colored glaze, some of which were cut into pieces and fitted into the recesses.

The other plaque bears the last several hieroglyphs of the name of Ramesses III on the sign for "gold." This tile employs a different technique. The recesses of the background tile are less deep and more clearly defined. The hieroglyphs are inlaid in a matte-finish faience with far greater precision than the bird tile, and the face of the hieroglyph tile has been glazed with a thinner and less reflective tan glaze. The technique of this tile is reminiscent of that used some 2,000 years earlier in the tomb chapel of Nefermaat (see no. 3). The tiles from Medinet Habu are closely paralleled by tiles of the same themes from the palace of Ramesses II at Kantir in the eastern Delta.

30.

FLORAL COLUMN

New Kingdom, Dynasty 20, reign of
Ramesses III, ca. 1182–1151 B.C.
Limestone, pigment
H: 43; W: 11 in (110 x 28 cm)
OIM 14089

THE EGYPTIANS' STRONG awareness of their environment was manifested by the incorporation of animals and plant elements into their art. Most architectural forms were based upon soft mediums such as reed matting and columns of reeds or timber that were transformed into imperishable stone.

Not only does this fragment of an elaborately decorated architectural element show organic materials (flowers) translated into stone, but the entire column is merely decorative, being carved in relief onto the surface of a slab of limestone. The decorative column represents an elaborate bouquet of flowers with their stems tied together. The uppermost blooms are red and blue lilies; the middle are blue papyrus flowers with yellow and red sepals; and the lowest blooms are blue and green lotuses nestled within yellow sepals. The shaft of the column is carved to represent the stems of the flowers. The lily stems have been cut shorter, exposing the inner group of stems.

As with so many examples of Egyptian art, the choice of the plants is symbolic. The papyrus was the emblematic plant of northern Egypt, the lily was the emblem of the southern region of the country. Here, they are physically united and securely lashed together. The king and his power and role in that unification may be alluded to by the rearing cobras, their hoods flared, with sun disks on their heads, that flank the papyrus blooms. A single uraeus tops a slender floral staff with papyrus capital shown to the left.

This column and a duplicate (now in the Egyptian Museum Cairo) originally flanked a statue niche in the western fortified gate of the temple of Ramesses III.

31.
GROOMING IMPLEMENTS

Razor with Case
New Kingdom, Dynasty 19,
ca. 1200 B.C.
Copper alloy, wood
Case: L: 5 1/8; W: 1 7/8; D: 3/4 in
(13.1 x 4.9 x 2 cm); Razor: L: 4 3/8;
W (overall): 3 1/8 in (10.7 x 8 cm)
OIM 10582

Hair Curler
New Kingdom, Dynasty 18,
ca. 1550–1293 B.C.
Copper alloy
L: 3 1/2; W: 1/2 in (9.2 x 1.3 cm)
OIM 9912

Ear Spoon
Roman Period, 1st century B.C.–
1st century A.D.
Bronze
L: 4 1/4 in (10.9 cm)
OIM 8515

Razor
New Kingdom, Dynasty 19,
ca. 1200 B.C.
Copper alloy
L: 4 3/4; W: 11/18 in (12.1 x 1.8 cm)
OIM 10502

Tweezers
Roman Period (?), 1st century B.C. (?)
Copper alloy
L: 2 3/4; W: 1/5 in (7.3 x 1.5 cm)
OIM 76

THE EGYPTIANS OF THE ELITE class were very conscientious about their grooming, with particular care being given to the appearance of the hair. Hairstyles changed dramatically from period to period. For example, short hair, which was fashionable for women in the Old Kingdom and the Late Period, was not as popular during the Middle and New Kingdoms. Both genders wore wigs and hair extensions to add volume to their natural hair. Mummies of women are often equipped with full wigs or with falls that were woven into their own hair, and hair was not uncommonly colored with henna. Hair on male mummies indicates that men did not, as recorded by Herodotus, always shave their head, the amount of hair apparently being dictated by individual taste and occupation.

Many tools associated with grooming have survived. The use of the hinged implement is not clear, but it is usually identified as a hair crimper or curler. It may have had several uses, for the handle is sharp, as if it could be used as a razor.

Most men were clean shaven, although in some periods they might wear a mustache or a goatee. Beards are only rarely encountered, and they are usually associated with men in mourning. Body hair was considered to be unclean, and men and women removed it with tweezers, sticky depilatories, and razors. The handle of the spatula-form razor here with its wooden case curves toward its sharpened cutting edge. By the New Kingdom the straight scalpel-form razor was also used.

32.

**STUDY FOR A ROYAL
TOMB PAINTING**

New Kingdom, Dynasty 20, reign of
Ramesses VI, ca. 1142–1134 B.C.
Limestone, pigment
H: 14 ½; W: 9 ¼; D: 2 ⅓ in
(37 x 23.7 x 6 cm)
OIM 17006

THE SKETCH ON THIS LARGE flake of smooth limestone shows a woman wearing a vulture cap topped with a flat crown with five floral elements. She wears a fine nearly transparent dress, with a sash tied at her waist and a broad collar necklace. In each hand she holds a scepter, terminating in the floral emblems of Upper and Lower Egypt. A rearing uraeus sits atop each scepter. The uraeus to the left wears the red crown of Lower Egypt; that to the right wears the white crown of Upper Egypt.

The headdress of this woman is rare. An early, possibly related version appears on the back of a chair of Satamun, daughter of Amunhotep III. In that example, the princesses' headdress is topped with five projections that terminate in floral umbels rather than with circles. That example bears a gazelle head, which was associated with royal women of lower rank, rather than the more conventional vulture head or uraeus. Another example, in the temple of Ramesses III at Medinet Habu, shows a woman, referred to as a Nefert ("a beautiful one") with a crown that seems to be a transition between the Satamun crown and the Chicago example. The Medinet Habu headdress is made up of a flat platform topped with four balls and three floral elements. Two examples which are very similar to that on the ostracon are found in the tombs of Nebet-tawy (tomb no. 60 dating to the reign of Ramesses II), and Tiyi (tomb no. 52 belonging to the mother of Ramesses IV) in the Valley of the Queens. The symbolism and significance of this complex and distinctive crown is unknown.

The similarity of the drawing on this ostracon to a scene in the tomb of Queen Isis (tomb no. 51), the mother of Ramesses VI, suggests that the ostracon may have been the preliminary sketch for a scene in that tomb. A great number of these preliminary sketches on ostraca are known. Many are thought to be the equivalent of artists' sketch pads, upon which the draftsman experimented with a design before transferring it to a wall (see no. 26). Other examples, such as number 27, are clearly finished pieces that were not intended for another purpose. As with many examples of Egyptian drawing and painting, one can see a preliminary outline in red pigment under the final black version of the drawing, particularly in the buttock and shoulder of the woman.

33.
HEAD OF A KING
Third Intermediate Period,
Dynasties 21–25, ca. 1070–664 B.C.
Baked clay and pigment
H: 1 3/16; W: 1 1/16; D: 1 1/8 in
(3.1 x 2.6 x 3 cm)
OIM 15554

ALTHOUGH THE MAJORITY of examples of Egyptian sculpture exhibited in museum galleries and illustrated in books are made of stone, bronze, or wood, Egyptian craftsmen also commonly used clay as a medium. From the New Kingdom onward, most baked clay sculptures were mold-made figures, sold to people as offerings or souvenirs when they visited temples. More rare in that era are individually hand-modeled figures such as this head which, through the uraeus on its forehead, indicates that it is supposed to represent a king. It is unknown if the tendril-like hair, the bulbous eyes, and slit-like mouth should be understood as a satirical comment on the king, or if this peculiar representation is simply a genre of informal folk art which is otherwise poorly attested. Informal—and unflattering—representations of the king are extremely rare, and if this example had not been excavated under controlled circumstances, it would certainly be dismissed as a bad forgery.

The head has traces of dark red powdery pigment that is common on other excavated terra-cotta figurines. The color is similar to that used on the skin of male figures (see nos. 7, 8), perhaps to indicate that their skin has been reddened by the sun. The same color is applied to many examples of clay figurines of women, although traditionally the skin area of statues and figurines of women was pigmented yellow.

During the excavation of Medinet Habu, a wide variety of baked clay figurines was recovered in forms of female figurines, women on beds, men with exaggerated genitalia, birds, dogs, and horses. It is tempting to imagine an ancient resident of Medinet Habu fashioning this small head from a bit of clay as he looked at formal representations of the king on the side of the temple.

34.

CANOPIC JARS

Third Intermediate Period,
Dynasty 22, ca. 800 B.C.

Limestone

Luxor, Deir el Bahari

2094 (Duamutef) H (overall): 13 ⁵/₈
D (jar): 4 ¹/₂ in (34.7 x 11 cm)

2092 (Qebehsenuef)
H (overall): 13 ¹/₂; (34.2 cm);
D (jar): 4 ⁷/₈ in (12.5 cm)

2093 (Hapi)
H (overall): 12 ³/₄; D (jar): 4 ³/₄ in
(32.3 x 12 cm)

2091 (Imsety) H (overall): 13 ¹/₂;
D (jar): 5 in (34.3 x 12.7 cm)

OIM 2091–94

CANOPIC JARS ARE RITUAL VESSELS for the storage of embalmed viscera removed from the body during the mummification process in the effort to promote the desiccation, and ultimately the preservation, of the body. Canopic jars were made in sets of four to accommodate the four major organs (stomach, liver, lungs, and intestines) that were removed. These organs were preserved in canopic jars rather than being discarded because it was believed that the deceased would be reborn in the afterlife, and that all elements of his or her body were required for rebirth.

Canopic jars could be made of terracotta, faience, or wood, but they are most commonly of limestone or Egyptian alabaster (calcite). They were made for royal and non-royal burials, as well as for the burials of Apis bulls who were sacred to the god Ptah. Canopic jars were normally stored in the tomb within chests or shrines made of wood, cartonnage, or stone.

The earliest set of canopic jars was found in the Giza tomb of Meresankh III, the wife of Menkaure (Dynasty 4, ca. 2530 B.C.). However, the tradition of removing viscera can be documented earlier in Dynasty 4 by niches in tombs that correspond to the placement of the later canopic jars, and by stone blocks with recesses for the viscera. The earliest examples of canopic jars have flat, dish-like lids. First Intermediate Period examples usually have four human heads, which, as indicated by the brief inscriptions on the jars, represent the deceased. By the Middle Kingdom, texts on the jars refer to protective deities called the Four Sons of Horus, indicating that the jars were associated with those gods rather than with the deceased. By early Dynasty 19 (ca. 1279 B.C.), this association of the jars with the Sons of Horus was so complete, that the jar stoppers thereafter normally took the form of the distinctive heads of those protective deities (falcon, ape, jackal, and human). Royal and non-royal examples tended to follow the same stylistic patterns, although the canopic containers from the tombs of Tutankhamun (Dynasty 18, ca. 1325 B.C.) and Shoshenq II (Dynasty 22, ca. 877–875 B.C.), as well as from a few non-royal burials, were anthropoid in imitation of the coffin in which the tomb owner was interred. Canopic jars continued to be used into the Ptolemaic Period (1st century B.C.). Although no examples have been dated to the early Roman Period (1st century B.C.–1st century A.D.), scenes of embalming rituals on coffins and on tomb walls commonly include canopic jars.

Canopic jars had symbolic importance in burials and were considered to be integral to a proper burial. Some canopic jars from the Old and Middle Kingdom were placed in tombs, although they were never actually used. In a similar fashion, in the Third Intermediate Period (Dynasties 21–24, ca. 1070–714 B.C.), the mummified internal organs of the deceased were usually returned to the thorax and abdomen of the mummy. Yet the tradition of including canopic jars with the tomb equipment was so firmly established that jars with no or little interior space, as is the case with the set shown here, were included in the tomb furnishings. This symbolic use of canopic jars is underscored by the production of very small jars that, although showing signs of having been used, could not have accommodated a full human organ. The assumption is that only a small symbolic sample of the organ was placed in the jar, and the rest of the tissue was discarded.

This set of uninscribed canopic jars was recovered from a badly disturbed archaeological context by Edouard Naville at the temple of Queen Hathsepsut at Deir el Bahari in Luxor. They are "dummy" jars, with removable stoppers, but only a small interior cavity. The lids represent (left to right) Duamutef (jackal) who protected the stomach, Qebehsenuef (falcon) who protected the intestines, Hapi (ape) who protected the lungs, and Imsety (human) who guarded the liver.

The name "canopic" is derived from Canopus, the pilot of the ship of the Greek hero Menelaeus, who was especially revered in the west Delta city of Canopus (near modern Abu Kir). According to Classical authors, Canopus was venerated in the form of a jar with a human head. That type of jar was erroneously equated with canopic jars with human heads, although they are functionally, and theologically, unrelated. The association between Canopus and a canopic jar is even more mistaken because the jars with human heads from the Roman Period represent not Canopus, but usually the god Osiris, or less frequently Anubis or Isis.

35

A PRIEST OF HATHOR
Third Intermediate Period,
Dynasties 22–23, ca. 946–714 B.C.
Limestone, pigment
H: 16; W: 9; D: 7 ³⁄₄ in
(41 x 23 x 20 cm)
OIM 10729

THIS STATUE OF A SEATED MAN, his cloak drawn down over his feet, represents a man named Basa. His arms, crossed in front of him, are suggested by a ridge on top of the statue. His hands, which emerge from the cloak, are visible above his knees. He grasps a handkerchief in his right hand. His left hand is placed flat on the top of his knee. Basa wears a blunt beard and a thick, blunt-cut wig with side-to-side striations indicating the hair.

The surface of the cloak as well as the back pillar is covered with texts and representations. On the front of the statue, Basa is shown to the right dressed in a priest's panther skin, with a ritual vessel (see no. 50) over his arm, adoring the gods Osiris and Isis. On the left and right shoulder of the statue, Basa is shown kneeling in adoration of Osiris.

The texts record the names and titles of twenty-six generations of Basa's father's family and four generations of his mother's family. Among Basa's titles are "Third Priest of Hathor," "Overseer of the Secrets of Clothing," "Investigating Scribe," "Astrologer," "Overseer of Cattle and Craftsmen," and "Temple Scribe at Dendera." He was a descendant of the well-known priest Nebwenenef who was buried at Thebes in the reign of Ramesses II. The text is one of the few records that documents Dendera and its priesthood during the early first millennium B.C.

Block statues appear first in Dynasty 12 (ca. 1976–1794 B.C.). They remain a feature of Egyptian art through the Late Period. It has been suggested that the seated pose emphasized the humility of man before god and that the tightly drawn cloak was an illusion to the wrappings of Osiris, and hence rebirth. Although such statues originally were made for tombs, by the New Kingdom they were also commissioned for placement in temples, where, it was believed, they would passively partake of the prayers offered to the gods.

For translation, see Ritner 1994, pp. 209-22, in Appendix 3.

36.
STELA OF THE HEARING EAR
Third Intermediate–Late Period,
Dynasties 22–26, ca. 946–525 B.C.
Limestone, pigment
H: 3 1/4; W: 2 3/16; D: 3/4 in
(8 x 5.7 x 2.1 cm)
OIM 16718

THIS SMALL, PORTABLE STELA is decorated with five pairs of human ears. Inscriptions on similar stelae indicate that the ears were thought to be the sympathetic ears of the god to whom prayers and petitions could be addressed. A variety of gods are associated with granting such petitions, and so it cannot be determined what god would be addressed. Prayers from a slightly earlier time, addressed to "any god by whom I pass," suggest that a great variety, or even all the gods, were considered to be able to help a petitioner.

These "hearing ear stelae" are known from at least the middle of Dynasty 18 (ca. 1350 B.C.). This example was excavated from the ruins of a private house, suggesting that it was part of a domestic cult. The practice of petitioning the gods for special favors or help was widespread in the New Kingdom and later. The great temples had places of petition, usually on the exterior back wall, where the common people could easily congregate. Some of these can be identified by the carving of ears on the walls, while others are simply referred to as "places of hearing petitions."

37.
OFFERING TO THE GOD
Third Intermediate Period,
Dynasty 22, ca. 946–735 B.C.
Wood, gesso, pigment
H: 9 ³/₄; W: 8 ¹/₂ in (25 x 22 cm)
OIM 1351

THIS FINELY PAINTED ROUND-TOP stela was one of a number of similar objects recovered from intrusive tombs located in the ruins of the temple of Ramesses II at Thebes. It portrays a woman named Djed-khonsu-iw-es-ankh ("Khonsu Said that She Will Live"), pouring a liquid offering for the seated god Re-Horakhty. She wears a linen dress edged with green and red fringe. It is not clear if the artist has allowed the body of the woman to show though the dress to emphasize her femininity, or if he was attempting to indicate that the linen was so fine that it was nearly transparent. Djed-khonsu-iw-es-ankh wears a broad collar necklace and a cone of scented fat on her head along with a lotus and mandrake or persea fruit, all of which were evocative of rebirth.

The god is seated on a multi-colored throne. He holds the crook and flail associated with kingship. The tall sign for "the west" is behind the god. The sign for "east" (damaged) is behind the woman.

The liquid offering is being poured upon a table of offerings laden with round loaves of bread, a beaker of dates (?), a bunch of grapes, a covered dish, two leeks, and a bouquet of flowers. Two situlae (see no. 50), vessels for milk or other liquid offerings, hang from the edges of the table. The winged disk with pendent uraei, a form of the god Behdeti, hovers over the scene.

Inscription:

An offering which the king gives [to] Re-Horakhty, the great god, lord of the heaven, that he [Re-Horakhty] may give invocation offerings of bread, beer, offerings, and provisions to the Osiris, the Mistress of the House, the noblewoman, Djed-khonsu-iw-es-ankh, justified, daughter of the Priest of Amun-Re, king of the gods, Chief of the Mysteries of the Clothing for the Divine Cult Statue, Ser-Djehuty.

38.

**CARTONNAGE CASE AND
MUMMY OF MERESAMUN**

Third Intermediate Period,
Dynasty 22, ca. 946–735 B.C.
Cartonnage (fabric, glue, plaster),
linen, pigment, human remains
H: 62 ³⁄₈ in (160 cm)
OIM 10797

THIS CARTONNAGE MUMMY CASE, which still contains a mummy, is inscribed with the name of Meresamun ("She lives for Amun"). This style of cartonnage coffin was formed over a temporary inner core made of mud and straw. After the coffin shell was completed, the core was scraped out and the wrapped mummy inserted into the case through the back and the back seam laced up. A separate footboard was attached, the entire case was covered with another layer of thin white plaster and then painted. The colored areas of the coffin were painted with a final layer of protective varnish that has turned yellow with age. This type of mummy case was normally part of a set of coffins composed of a wooden anthropoid (human-shaped) coffin, or even a series of two or three nested coffins, all of which would have been painted with religious scenes.

Meresamun is shown wearing the vulture headdress (see no. 56). The torso of the coffin is painted with scenes that allude to life after death and which were intended to ensure Meresamun's successful rebirth. Her chest is covered with the representation of layers of wide floral necklaces—symbols of regeneration. Below, to the right and left are two pairs of gods who were entrusted with the protection of the internal organs that were removed during the mummification process. These gods also appear on the lids of canopic jars, the containers in which the embalmed viscera were stored. To the right are the hawk-headed god, Qebehsenuef who guarded the intestines, and the jackal-headed Duamutef who guarded the stomach. To the left is the human-form Imsety who guarded the liver, and the ape-headed Hapi who guarded the lungs.

Between and slightly below these gods is a large representation of the falcon god Horus (or, perhaps, Re), with the sun's disk on his head, clasping a round *shen* ("eternity") sign in each talon. A feather fan, a symbol of divinity, emerges from each *shen* sign. The solar Horus, as a symbol of the eternally reborn sun, signified rebirth.

On either side of the central band on the leg area of the coffin are *wedjat* eyes, which symbolized health and regeneration. Behind the eyes are winged serpents with sun disks on their heads—symbols of protection. The serpent to the right hovers above the hieroglyphs for eternity, life, and dominion. Below the serpents are rams which functioned on several different levels. They may be a pun for the word "soul" (both the word "soul" and "ram" sounded the same in the ancient Egyptian language). The ram may also represent the god Khnum, one of the primary creator gods, Re, a solar deity, or Ba-neb-djed, who was associated with the soul of Osiris, one of the deities of the afterlife.

Larger scale hieroglyphs cover the lower leg area. To the right of the central band of hieroglyphs is the *djed* pillar, which symbolized the backbone of the god Osiris, the main deity of the afterlife and the deceased's association with that god in the afterlife. To the left is the *tiet* (so-called "Isis knot"), a symbol with broad meaning, associated generally with health and well-being. Two images of the jackal god Wepwawet, protector of the necropolis, decorate the upper surface of the feet. The footboard of the coffin is decorated with a bull which, on other coffins, is explicitly identified as the god Apis.

Where Meresamun lived and died is unknown, although the style of the coffin suggests that she was originally from the Theban (modern Luxor) area. According to the inscription, she held the title "Singer in the Interior of the Temple of Amun," a high position in the bureaucracy of priestesses. Many of the women who held this title were known to come from the best families of Thebes, and some of them served as attendants to the ruling family.

The coffin has never been opened and the mummy has never been unwrapped. In 1991, the mummy of Meresamun was examined by CT scans (computed tomography or "CAT"). During that study, radiologists suggested, on the basis of her teeth and bones, that she may have been about 30 years old at the time of her death. This was not considered to be an old age for an upper class woman of the period. However, the cause of her premature death is unknown.

Inscription:

A gift which the king gives to Re-Horakhty-Atum, Lord of the Two Lands and Heliopolis [and to] Ptah-Sokar-Osiris, Lord of Shechet, and Wennefer (a form of Osiris), Lord of the Sacred Land (i.e., the Necropolis), the great god, lord of heaven that he may give funerary offerings to the Osiris, the Singer in the Interior of the Temple of Amun, Meresamun, the one beneficial to Amun, justified.

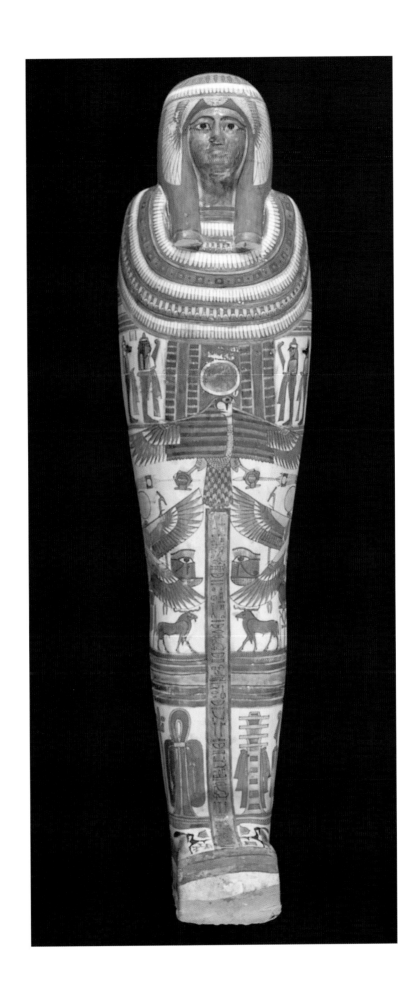

39.
BRICK STAMP

New Kingdom–Third Intermediate
Period, Dynasties 19–22,
ca. 1292–735 B.C.
Bronze
H: 4 ³/₈; W: 1 ⁵/₈; D (handle): ³/₄ in
(11.3 x 4.2 x 2 cm)
OIM 11171

THE ANCIENT EGYPTIANS gave proper names to buildings, and even to elements of buildings, such as doorways. For example, the name of the pyramid of King Userkaf at Sakkara was "Pure are the Places of Userkaf," and the mortuary temple of Thutmose IV at Thebes was "Thutmose is the Rightful Ruler." Mud bricks produced for a particular building project were often impressed with a stamp bearing the name of the structure for which it was produced.

This stamp, in the form of an oval topped by two feather plumes, bears the inscription "Hathor in Imu." Imu, known today as Kom el Hisn, is located in the west central delta. The site is poorly preserved, but textual sources indicate that the goddess Hathor was the principle deity of the town. This bronze stamp may have been employed to mark the bricks used in that temple.

Few examples of brick stamps survive. The impression that would have been left by this stamp has the same general dimensions as impressions recorded on actual bricks. Other examples of impressions on bricks (from Thebes) are also topped with double plumes. A strap-like piece of bronze is soldered to its reverse side to act as a handle.

40.

**AMUNIRDIS I AND
DIESE-HEB-SED**

Third Intermediate–Late Period,
Dynasties 25–26, ca. 656 B.C.
Sandstone, pigment
H: 19 1/8; L: 24 3/4; D: 7 3/8 in
(49 × 63.4 × 18.5 cm)
OIM 14681

THIS FRAGMENT OF SANDSTONE relief shows two women; Diese-heb-sed to the left and the God's Wife of Amun, Amunirdis I, to the right. Both women wear fine, almost transparent linen gowns and sandals with looped toes (see no. 57). Diese-heb-sed wears a heavy tripartite wig, while the God's Wife wears the vulture head-dress topped by a flat modius that would have supported two tall plumes. Inscriptions from other sources indicate that Diese-heb-sed was an attendant of Amunirdis. In that subservient role, she stands with her arms passively at her sides as Amunirdis raises her hands in adoration of the deity who was once shown to the right.

In the era in which this relief was carved, Egypt was ruled by Nubian kings who installed their daughters to be their representatives in Thebes. Amunirdis was the daughter of the Nubian pharaoh Taharka, one of the greatest of the Kushite rulers. The God's Wives were considered to be married to the god Amun, a deity who had special associations with the state and the concept of kingship. These women were assisted in the affairs of state by a great number of Egyptian administrators. Diese-heb-sed, whose title was "Singer in the Interior of the Temple of Amun" was a lower ranking member of the temple personnel. She is also shown with Amunirdis in a chapel at the Karnak Temple, suggesting that she may have been a personal attendant of the God's Wife.

Diese-heb-sed came from a well-known family. Her brother was the mayor of Thebes, Montuemhet, one of the highest ranking administrators of the area (see no. 41). This fragment may have come from the now destroyed tomb chapel of Diese-heb-sed at Medinet Habu.

Inscription:
. . . the eastern horizon, kissing the earth for the westerners (i.e., the deceased ones). . . [Singer in the Interior of the temple of Amun Diese-heb]-sed, daughter of the Priest of Amun, the Scribe of the Offering table. . . [Nes-ptah]. . . that you may traverse the heaven as one justified.

41.

RELIEFS FROM THE TOMB OF MONTUEMHET

Third Intermediate-Late Period, Dynasties 25–26, 656 B.C.
Limestone, pigment
OIM 17973: H: 9 5/8; W: 20 1/2 in (24.7 x 52.7 cm)
OIM 17974-5: H: 17; W: 40 in (43.1 x 101.6 cm)
OIM 18828: H: 8 5/8; W: 6 1/4 in (21.8 x 15.8 cm)

THESE FRAGMENTS OF PAINTED and carved limestone once decorated the tomb of the "Fourth Priest of Amun, the Mayor of Thebes," Montuemhet in Luxor. Over the last century, pieces of the wall relief have been dispersed to museums throughout the world. The fine white limestone, interesting compositions, and excellent workmanship make the reliefs from this tomb among the best from ancient Egypt. They are particularly interesting for the way that they adopt and imitate themes from earlier periods of Egyptian history.

Most of the Chicago fragments deal with the production and conveyance of funerary offerings to the tomb of the mayor. One, OIM 17973 shows a boat laden with two large baskets of fruit destined for the funerary feast. Oarsmen sit at the bow and stern. The captain, equipped with his staff of office, raises his arm, and points his index finger, either to show the way, or in a gesture of magical protection known from Old Kingdom river scenes. The fish and the water under the ship are indicated in paint alone, perhaps a labor saving device.

Another fragment (OIM 17974–5), preserves the top and bottom of two different registers. The upper shows the netting of fish. The long seine net, its top floating on triangular shaped floats, its bottom weighted down with thin sinkers, is being pulled in by men standing on shore at the water's edge. The curved end of the rope can be seen above the net. In a whimsical touch, a tilapia fish (left) has evaded the net by hiding behind a water lily. The fish in the net have been rendered in great detail and can be identified, left to right, as a parrot-fish (*Petrocephalus*), a carp (*Barbus bynni*), two catfish (*Claris*), and a tilapia.

In the lower register of the same fragment is a procession of women who carry baskets of food offerings to the tomb. The hieroglyphs before each woman identify the contents of their baskets: (left to right) trussed fowl; all (kinds) of bread; figs; garden produce; persea (?) fruit; meat and cakes, followed by "for" Montuemhet, whose name is preceded by one of his titles.

The partially preserved scene on fragment OIM 18828 is an animated depiction of two girls, pulling each other's hair. The section of a large basket above the girls, the sheaves of grain, and the small basket between the girls indicate that the scene is part of a harvest scene in conjunction with the production of food offerings. The girl on the left is apparently naked, other than for a decorative belt, although parallels for this scene suggest that she may also have worn a diaphanous garment also in paint. This scene is a copy of a painting in the nearby tomb of the courtier Menna who lived some 800 years before the time that Montuehmet's tomb was built. This tendency to copy earlier motifs and to imitate earlier styles is a major feature of the art of Dynasties 25 and 26.

Late Period

(664–332 B.C.)

42.

STATUE OF AMUN
Late Period, Dynasty 26, reign of
Amasis, 570–526 B.C.
Bronze, gilt
H: 9 3/8 (24 cm); Base: L: 7 3/8;
W: 3 3/4; D: 1 1/8 in (19 x 9.5 x 2.8 cm)
OIM 10584

THIS STATUE PORTRAYS the god Amun seated on a separately made throne. He wears the curved false beard that symbolizes his divinity and a flat-topped crown that would have supported two tall plumes and a sun disk. His left hand is clasped near the top of his knee. The other holds fragments of a staff. Armlets of thin gold foil adorn his upper arms.

The sides of the throne are decorated with feather patterns. The back of the throne is detailed with an inverted papyrus and lotus pattern, as if the top of the fabric seat cover was looped up over the back of the chair, presenting the pattern upside down.

The date of this piece and its historical importance are securely fixed by an inscription on its base that states that it was dedicated during the lifetime of

Nitocris II, the daughter of King Amasis. Throughout Egyptian history, but especially in the middle years of the first millennium B.C., women of the royal family held very high positions in the theocratic bureaucracies in Thebes (see no. 40). The inscription relates that Nitocris II held the office of "First Priest of Amun," a post that gave her primacy in the ranks of the priests of Amun and which presumably gave her authority over the vast economic holdings of the temple of Amun. The office had previously been held by Ankh-nes-nefer-ib-re, a daughter of King Psamtik II. She also held the title "Adoratress of the God," and, as attested elsewhere, "God's Wife of Amun," the highest offices in the Theban theocratic administration.

We know very little about Nitocris II. Although the inscription states that her father was King Amasis and that her mother was Ankh-nes-nefer-ib-re, it is known that the name of Amasis' wife was Tentheta. The presence of two mothers, one adoptive (Ankh-nes-nefer-ib-re) and one biological (Tentheta), is well attested among the God's Wives who employed adoption as a means of passing land holdings and wealth connected with their office to their successor, who may not have been in a direct line of inheritance. In this case, the senior partner transferred only the title "First Priest of Amun," which, before the time of Ankh-nes-nefer-ib-re, had always been held by a man. The respective duties of the offices of God's Wife and First Priest of Amun are not well understood, but placing both posts in the hands of royal princesses is an indication of the economic authority of the royal family at that time. The office of God's Wife and Adoratress of the God are no longer attested after the Persian invasion in 525 B.C.

The inscription on the sides of the base indicates that the statue was dedicated in honor of Amun by, or for, a "Singer in the Interior of the Temple of Amun" named Ankh-nes-nefer-ib-re. Because that title was not born by the God's Wives, and since the personal name is not enclosed in a cartouche (as on the top of the base), it should be assumed that this Ankh-nes-nefer-ib-re is a different person than the God's Wife of the same name.

Inscriptions:

Sides of base: Words said by Amun-Re, Lord of the Thrones of the Two Lands, who loves Thebes, as he gives life, rejuvenation and health, a [long] lifetime and great [praises], sweetness of heart and happiness every day, [with] eyes seeing and ears hearing, for the Singer in the Interior of the [Temple of] Amun, Ankh-nes-nefer-ib-re. . . . daughter of. . .justified.

Top of base: Amun-Re, Lord of the Thrones of the Two Lands, who loves Thebes, protector of the [First] Priest of Amun Nitocris, daughter of the Lord of the Two Lands, Amasis. May he live! Her mother is the Divine Adoratress Ankh-nes-nefer-ib-re. May she live!

43.
STELA OF HARSIESE
Late Period, Early Dynasty 26,
ca. 664 B.C.
Wood, gesso, pigment
H: 16 ³/₄; W: 13 ³/₈; D: ³/₄ in
(43.3 x 34.4 x 1.8 cm)
OIM 12220

THIS STELA SHOWS the priest of the god Montu, Harsiese adoring the gods Re-Horakhty (left) and Atum (right). As was common with private stelae of this period, the dedicator is shown on the extreme left and right within a colorful frame that represents the perimeter of a temple or shrine. At the top of the stela, Behdeti, a creator god represented by a great winged disk, hovers below the vault of heaven which is delimited by a frieze of heavenly stars.

To the left, Harsiese, with shaven head and a mid-calf kilt covered with the panther cloak of a priest, raises his hands in adoration of the falcon-headed god Re-Horakhty. A cone of perfumed fat—a symbol of purification—rests on his head. A low table heaped with gutted fowl and round and tall loaves of bread for the god stands between Harsiese and the deity. A large lotus, an emblem of rebirth, is placed atop the food offerings. Re-Horakhty wears a tight fitting garment with shoulder straps fastened with a knot. He carries the hieroglyphs for life and dominion. To the right, Harsiese, dressed in the same manner, but here wearing a heavy wig with a perfume cone, and a short false beard, adores the god Atum who wears the double crown.

The imagery and the text (Spell 15 from the Book of the Dead) below the representations are an extended reference to rebirth by the deceased following in the path of the eternal cycle of the sun. The god Re-Horakhty on the left was mythologically equated with the new sun that was reborn at the break of day, while Atum was associated with the setting sun. In the text of the stela, Harsiese's name is associated with that of Osiris, the god of the afterlife, indicating that he has been reborn in the realm of the gods. A stela such as this might have been placed in a local temple to commemorate the deceased.

Inscriptions:

Lunette: Behdeti, the Great God.

Left: The God's Father, beloved of the god, Seeker of the Sound Eye, Harsiese, justified. Re-Horakhty.

Lower Left: Words said by this Priest of Montu, Lord of Thebes, the Osiris, Harsiese, justified, son of the Robing Priest, Ankh-ef-en-khonsu the elder, justified, "Hail to you when you rise in your horizon as Re satisfied with Maat! You have crossed the sky and everyone sees you. When you have gone and are hidden from their face(s), you place yourself in the underworld every day. People prosper when they row your majesty, for your rays are in their face(s), although unrecognized. There is nothing of electrum, there is not one who reports. . ."

Right: Atum. The priest, Adorer of the God, Harsiese, justified.

Lower Right: Words said by this priest of Montu, the Lord of Thebes, the Osiris, Harsiese, justified, born of the Mistress of the House, Mut-hotep, justified, "Hail to you who has come as Atum, having become the creator of the gods! Hail to you who has come (as) holy spirits who are in the west! Hail to you foremost of the gods who illuminates the underworld with his beauty! Hail to you who conveys the blessed, who rows as he who is in his disk! Hail to you who are greater than the (other) gods, who arises in the heaven and who rules the underworld!"

44.

DONATION STELA

Late Period, Dynasty 26, reign of
Necho II, 599 B.C.
Limestone
H: 19 ½; W: 11 ⅓; D: 3 ⅛ in
(50 x 29 x 8 cm)
OIM 13943

THE TEXT ON THIS STELA records that King Necho II made a donation of halfa grass to the temple of Thoth in Busiris (modern Abu Sir in the Delta), in order to maintain a lamp that burned in that temple. Such transfers, referred to as donation decrees, are a prominent feature of the Egyptian economy. In ancient Egypt, all land ostensibly belonged to the king, who granted its use to temples and individuals. Such land grants were made in return for service to the state, in connection with state offices, or for the maintenance of temples. The holder of the land could profit from its productivity, or from sub-letting it, yet the state maintained actual ownership of the real estate.

In the decree on this stela, the produce grown on a particular estate was transferred from one recipient to another. In precise bureaucratic fashion, the administrator of the temple of Thoth, Djed-thoth-iu-ef-ankh, who received the grant, is named. Another man, Pa-di-neshmet, son of Kherem-hor, "who came concerning" the grass, may have been in charge of the lands upon which it was grown. The curse at the end of the text is typical of many legal documents.

The upper portion of the stela shows a small figure of Necho II, dressed in a kilt with the bull's tail that symbolized his power, and the double crown, presenting the hieroglyph for "field" to three gods. The god directly before the king is Osiris, the principle god of the city of Busiris. The unnamed goddess behind Osiris is probably his wife Isis. The ibis-headed god Thoth, whose temple was the beneficiary

of the endowment, is shown to the left. The lunette is filled with a large winged disk representing the god Behdeti over a thin, curved, hieroglyph for "sky."

Unlike most stelae on which the text is carefully spaced, here it stops two thirds of the way through the last line. The blank section at the bottom of the stela suggests that it was inserted into a base for display to serve as a reminder of the royal gift to the temple. It is not known under whose reign the cartouches of Necho were defaced.

Inscription:

Year 11, under the majesty of the Horus, the perceptive one, the Two Ladies, justified, Golden Horus, beloved of the gods, [Wehemibre], Son of Re, [Necho], living forever. His majesty donates this halfa grass of [the estate of] Pa-en-na-mesw in the Busirite nome to maintain a lamp of Thoth, bull of the great temple in Busiris, under the authority of the Doorkeeper of Thoth, Djed-thoth-iu-ef-ankh, son of Padihor by Pa-di-neshmet, son of Kheremhor who came concerning it. (As for) any scribe or official or any man or anyone who shall come to the field to take (from it), or to do things in it on earth, his name shall not exist on earth, his son and daughter shall not grow up on earth, and he shall not be buried in the necropolis.

45.
COMPOSITE DEITY
Late Period, Dynasties 26–31,
ca. 664–332 B.C.
Bronze
H: 5 5/8 (14.5 cm); Base: L: 2 5/8;
W: 2 1/4; H: 3/4 in (6.8 x 5.9 x 1.8 cm)
OIM 11375

THIS GOD REPRESENTS the fusion of several deities, the result being a fantastic being with special protective powers. He has two faces; that looking forward is of the jackal god Anubis, that to the back is a falcon, the symbol of Re or Horus. His tail is forked and feathered like that of a falcon. He holds cobras in each hand, a pair of vultures emerge from his knees, and he stands on a pair of crocodiles which are encircled by another serpent.

Throughout their history, the Egyptians had a predilection to combine deities into composites such as Amun-Re, or Ptah-Sokar-Osiris, that were honored alongside the uncombined forms. This syncretistic tendency became a strong element in religion in the Late Period, and often the individual elements of the resulting combinations cannot be identified.

The cobras in the hands, the vultures from the knees, and the crocodiles under the god's feet function on several different levels of symbolism. On one hand, these are wild, untamed animals of the desert—archetypal symbols of danger. Yet, they were considered to have ambivalent natures—the snake Apophis was the ultimate evil god, yet a great snake, Mehen (no. 2), protected the sun god in the dark hours of the night and a protective serpent, the uraeus, appeared on the forehead of the king. An animal's dangerous aspect could be mastered by a superior god. In this case, the composite god stands upon the crocodiles and immobilizes the snakes in his grasp, a feat that is referred to in magical spells: "Every male and female serpent, every snake, every lion, every crocodile is under the feet of this god," and thereby neutralized. This theme of mastering and trampling animals is related to scenes of the king trampling upon his foreign enemies, a theme that was employed throughout all of the pharaonic period and persisted into the Byzantine era.

The mastery of animals was not the only way that their evil nature could be subdued. Other Egyptian magical texts refer to turning evil against evil and to the subjugation of animals serving as allies against their own kind. Hence the subjugated snakes and crocodile would protect against the bite of those same creatures.

Statuettes and amulets of composite deities conquering and allying themselves with evil animals were intended to protect against the bite and sting of wild animals and to generally protect against evil.

46.

DEMOTIC "MARRIAGE" PAPYRUS

Late Period, Dynasty 30, year 17 of Nectanebo I (December 365–64 B.C.)

Papyrus, pigment

L: 97 ½; W: 14 ⅕ in (230 x 37 cm)

OIM 17481

THIS TEXT IS AMONG THE earliest known examples in demotic script of what is commonly referred to as a "marriage contract," a legal document that specified both spouses' property rights. Egypt was among the rare cultures in the ancient world in which women could inherit, hold, and transfer property separately from their husbands, and so contracts were drawn up to specify not only what property may have been brought into the marriage, but also its disposition in case of divorce or death.

The text details the holdings of the husband and the disposition of his property among children who may be born to him by his wife, named Peset, and also directly to his wife in the case of divorce. Among the provisions of the endowment are: "There belongs to the children which you will bear to me everything which I possess and that I shall acquire, house, field, courtyard, building plot, male servant, female servant, all animals and all title, deed and contract in the world that I possess." If the couple divorces, the woman is promised a certain ration of grain and amounts of silver "for your yearly sustenance and clothing at whatever dwelling you have preferred."

Such documents were themselves not legal proof of marriage nor a requisite for marriage. Certainly not every couple commissioned such a document, for the role of such contracts was the regulation of property and the patterns of inheritance of jointly or solely held property. Marriage in ancient Egypt was a relatively informal matter that consisted mainly of a man and woman living together, ideally in their own household. There was little shame in divorce. Either partner could institute divorce, and thereafter both were free to remarry. The brief genealogy given for the man and his wife indicate that they were half brother and sister, an arrangement that may have been favored for keeping family fortunes intact.

The reverse of the papyrus is inscribed with a list of thirty-six witnesses. Some of them list their professions, or the professions of their father, such as "Scribe," "Deputy of Sobek," and "God's Father." The document states that any changes to it made by the woman or a witness could be sworn only "in the building in which are the judges."

The document is made of twelve joined sheets of overlapped strips of papyrus fibers. It is inscribed on both sides in the elegant cursive script called demotic that was used to write the ancient Egyptian language from about 600 B.C. to A.D. 450. The script is written from right to left. The large decorative hieroglyph for "year" that begins the document is like an uncial capital; it begins the phrase; "Year 17 [month] Paopi of pharaoh, life, prosperity, and health, Nectanebo."

For translation, see Nims 1958, pp. 239–40, and Jasnow 1997, pp. 11–12 in Appendix 3.

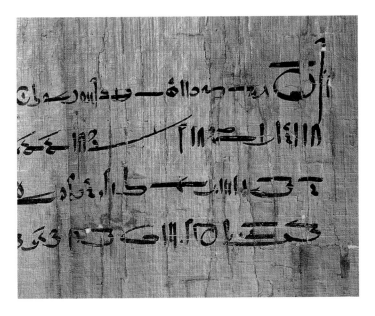 

47.

HEAD FROM A CAT COFFIN

Late Period, Dynasties 26–31,
664–332 B.C.
Bronze
H: 6 ¼; W: 4 ¾; D: 4 ½ in
(16 x 12.2 x 11.7 cm)
OIM 18826

THIS FINE REPRESENTATION of a cat's head once decorated a coffin for a mummified feline. Although many such "cat masks" are known, no examples have been found *in situ*, and it has been suggested that they were attached to the outside of a wooden coffin, much in the manner in which human coffins had a human face and hands attached in high relief.

The practice of widespread animal sacrifice in connection with the veneration of gods appeared in the late second millennium B.C. and reached a zenith in the Ptolemaic Period (4th–1st centuries B.C.). The sacrificed animal was an avatar of the deity of the temple, but the animal itself was not considered to be sacred. Many types of animals were sacrificed. Cats were associated with the goddesses Bastet and Sekhmet, baboons and ibises were sacred to the god Thoth, hawks and falcons symbolized Horus, and dogs and jackals were associated with Anubis. Animal sacrifice was a very common practice, as attested by the ibis catacombs at North Sakkara that are estimated to hold the remains of more than four million bird mummies. The animals kept specifically for this purpose were raised by temple workers in pens near the temple to the particular deity. X-ray examination of mummified cats has indicated that the majority were about ten months old at death, and that most were killed by having their neck wrung. They were then mummified. Some were carefully wrapped in elaborate bandages, and some even have ears and faces molded in linen. Some were encased in wood or bronze coffins, and others in simple pottery jars. Once prepared, the mummy was sold to a pilgrim who visited the temple. The visitor then donated it to the temple as a sign of his or her piety. The animal mummy was eventually placed in a catacomb or communal grave. This practice was an important source of revenue for the temples.

Cat cemeteries are known from many locations in Egypt, but the main cult center of the deity Bastet was at Bubastis (Tell Basta) in the northeast Delta. The catacombs were known as "the resting place of the cats."

48.

ORACULAR STATUE IN THE FORM OF A FALCON

Late Period, Dynasties 26-31, 664-332 B.C.

Serpentine (beak is modern restoration)

H: 23 ¼; W (breast): 9 ¼; D (base): 21 ⅞ in (59.6 x 23.4 x 55.9 cm)

OIM 10504

THIS STATUE OF A FALCON represents the god Horus. The legs are carved with an indication of scales, but there is little definition of the feathers. The eye sockets have traces of a black mastic-like substance that would have secured pupils. Other contemporary statues of falcons suggest that the bird originally wore a double crown.

A hole runs from the tail of the bird through the body to the crown, then down to the beak. It is unclear if the purpose of this considerable undertaking was to connect the underside and invisible part of the bird to the beak, or to connect the underside to the beak and the top of the head. Since the channel does not appear to have any structural use, it must be functional, perhaps in association with delivering oracles. Some Late Period oracles employed statues of animals, some of which were thought to give their decision not through nodding, as with many New Kingdom oracles, but by actually speaking. Several other statues associated with oracles have holes bored through them, presumably to allow the voice of the priest to reach the petitioner. A statue of the falcon god Re-Horakhty and one of the deified Queen Arsinoe were bored out in a manner similar to this falcon. The base for an oracle statue excavated at Kôm el Wist (near Alexandria) was found to be connected to what has been taken to be a bronze "speaking tube" that relayed the voice of priests to the petitioner. Similar ways of allowing unseen priests to become involved in oracles have been noted at temples at Karanis, Kom Ombo, and Dendera.

The heavy brow ridge of the falcon, the lack of detail in the feathers, and the markings on the face suggest that this sculpture dates to the Late Period rather than to the New Kingdom, as has previously been suggested. Its proposed use as an oracle would also indicate a Late Period date.

49.

THOTH EMBLEM

Late Period, Dynasties 26–31,
664–332 B.C.

Glazed faience

H: 6 ⁵⁄₈; W: 3; D: 5 ½ in
(17.2 x 7.7 x 14.1 cm)

OIM 10101

THIS ENIGMATIC OBJECT represents an offering that is shown in temple offering scenes from late Dynasty 18 (ca. 1350 B.C.) into the Roman Period. It represents a baboon, a form of the god Thoth. His torso and flexed legs have been rendered as the stylized hieroglyph that is commonly used in other contexts to represent seated gods (see no. 51). Long locks, or plaits, descend from the ape's brow down his mid-back, cascading over his mane which, based on other examples, is indicated by a series of incised lines. The ape rests against a pillar, the top of which, to judge from other intact examples, may originally have been forked. The platform upon which he rests is a stylized basket decorated with a central diamond pattern filled with a floral pattern that is the hieroglyph for "festival."

Although the origins of this composition are obscure, it is associated with time and time keeping. Bronze instruments that measured time by the passage of water, using the same principle as an hourglass filled with sand, are known from the Ptolemaic and Roman Periods. They are composed of a rectangular column with a baboon seated at its base. On this Thoth emblem, that column is represented by the pillar—which is the hieroglyph *hen*, meaning "time." The baboon god Thoth was traditionally associated with the reckoning of time, and he is also used to decorate large vessels that functioned as water clocks (see no. 55).

Temple reliefs that show the king presenting a Thoth emblem to the gods apparently symbolized the ruler's eternal commitment to maintain the land on behalf of the gods. It is possible that this statue was originally part of the furnishings of a temple, and that it was employed in such a ceremony. Although a score of these statuettes are known, very few have a sure provenance or a well-defined date.

50.

RITUAL VESSEL (SITULA)

Late Period, Dynasties 26–31,
664–332 B.C.
Copper alloy
H (overall): 12 ⅛; H (of vessel): 7 ⅞;
D (of rim): 2 ¼; Maximum D: 5 ½ in
(30.7 x 19.8 x 5.7 x 13.9 cm)
OIM 11394

C O O L   W A T E R   W A S   O N E of the most important funerary offerings, for it was thought that the deceased needed refreshing beverages in the afterlife. A category of funerary priests, called *wah mu*, later referred to as choachyte, were engaged to pour water libations in funerary rituals. Such offerings were most commonly held in handled buckets called situlae. This example is incised with a scene of a priest of Montu named Pen-maa offering to his deceased mother. With his right hand, he pours water onto a low offering table in the form of the hieroglyph for "offering." He holds a long incense burner in his left hand. The handle of the incense burner is decorated with a hawk head. Its other end is in the form of a human hand that holds the smoking incense cup.

Pen-maa wears a long skirt under a leopard skin cloak, the standard garb of funerary priests. His mother, whose name is Ta-baket-en-ese, is shown seated before a table of offerings stacked with tall loaves of bread. She holds a handkerchief, a frequent pose of unclear symbolism, in her left hand. The hieroglyphic text that covers most of the surface of the situla is Utterance 32 from the Pyramid Texts, a body of religious recitations that was compiled nearly 2,000 years before this situla was inscribed.

Inscriptions:

Recitation: This cool water of yours Oh Osiris foremost of the Westerners, the great god, Lord of Abydos— this cool water of the Osiris-Ta-baket-en-ese, justified, daughter of the Priest of Montu, Lord of Thebes, Overseer of the Cattle (?) Padi-Amun-nefer-hetep, justified, her mother being the Mistress of the House Nesy-hor—has gone forth to your son, has gone forth to Horus. I have come bringing to you the eye of Horus that your heart may be refreshed by it, bringing it under your two sandals. Take to yourself the flow that comes forth for you. You heart will not be weary with it. Recite four times: come that you might come forth at the voice!

Above priest: His *[sic]* son, the Priest of Montu in Thebes, Pen-maa, presenting incense and liquid offerings.

51.

BOOK OF THE DEAD

Late Period, Dynasty 31–early
Ptolemaic Period, 4th century B.C.
Papyrus, pigment
H: 14 3/4; L: 360 in (37.5 x 914 cm)
OIM 9787

THIS SECTION FROM a Book of the Dead belonging to a man named Neysu-shu-tefnut, the son of Sep-en-hor and Esereshti, shows Chapter 125, the weighing of the heart. According to Egyptian funerary beliefs, the heart of the deceased was weighed before a tribunal of the gods to verify his or her moral goodness. If the deceased passed the judgment, he or she would be reborn in the afterlife.

This section of the papyrus depicts Osiris, the god of the underworld, seated in a shrine placed within a larger shrine with a decorated top. Before him in the upper register are the forty-two Gods of the Hall of Two Truths—the judges of the dead—all of whom except one, wear a feather, the symbol of truth, on their heads. To the lower right is the deceased, wearing the sash of a priest, saluting Maat, the goddess of truth. Dominating the area in the center of the vignette is the scale upon which the heart of the deceased (shown as a small vessel in the right pan) is weighed against the small figure of Maat. The falcon-headed god Horus, and Anubis, the guardian of the necropolis, guard the scale, while Thoth, the god who records the outcome, is represented both by the seated baboon on top of the scale and by the ibis-headed figure who stands with his raised ink palette and pen. Between Thoth and Osiris is a stand that supports the terrible monster, Ammet—part crocodile, part lion—who will swallow the heart of the unjust. Above Ammet are the Four Sons of Horus who guard the viscera of the deceased.

The papyrus employs both hieroglyphic and hieratic scripts. The more formal hieroglyphs were used as captions for the representations, a pairing found in Egyptian reliefs. The more cursive hieratic was employed for the longer text that was not associated with the vignette. The name of the deceased is neatly integrated into the hieratic text, yet it has been omitted from the hieroglyphic text accompanying the judgment scene. This suggests that the papyrus may have been purchased with the vignette already painted, and that the hieratic text was added later by a different scribe working on a special commission for Neysu-shu-tefnut. Several corrections in the hieratic text indicate that the second scribe carefully checked his work.

Neysu-shu-tefnut was a fairly low level priest who served as "Priest of Khonsu," "Priest of the Falcons who live in the Sacred Tree," "Priest of the Great Foundation," and "Fourth Priest of Osiris."

For translation of this vignette of the papyrus, see Allen 1960, pp. 202-03, in Appendix 3.

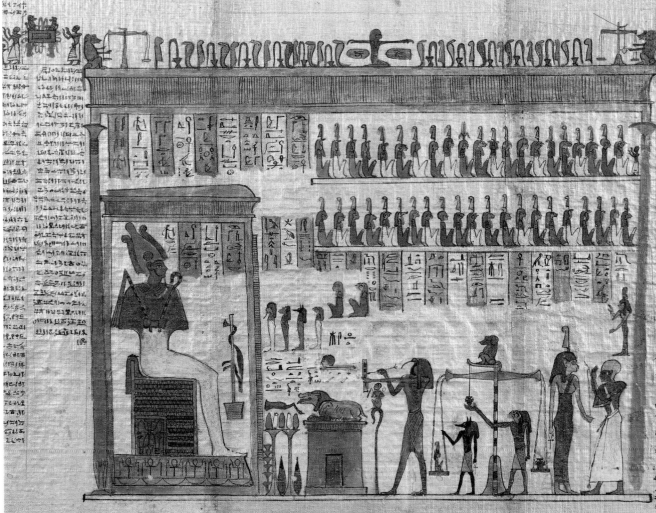

Ptolemaic, Roman, and Byzantine Periods

(4TH CENTURY B.C.–8TH CENTURY A.D.)

52.
STATUE BASE OF DJED-HOR

Early Ptolemaic Period
(Macedonian Dynasty), reign of
Philip Arrhidaeus, ca. 323–317 B.C.
Basalt
L: 22; W: 13; H: 12 ³⁄₈ in
(56.2 x 33.5 x 32 cm)
OIM 10589

THIS BLOCK, WHICH ONCE held a statue in the recess on its top, was commissioned by a man named Djed-hor, the "Doorkeeper of Horus Khenty-Khety" and "Chief Guardian of the Falcon with All his Goods" who worked in a temple at Athribis caring for sacred falcons.

The right side of the base is incised with a scene of Djed-hor in the company of his seven sons. Their heads are shaven in the manner of priests. The name of each son, with the name of his father and mother, is given. The opposite side of the base shows the female side of the family with Djed-hor. Four daughters are shown, as are two different, presumably consecutive, wives. Each woman carries a pair of rattles called sistra. The sistra in their left hands are topped with a shrine-shaped structure; those in their right hands bear a Hathor head under the plain loop. The areas not devoted to the scenes of Djed-hor and his family are covered with incised hieroglyphs that relate his accomplishments and his devotion to the gods.

From these texts we know that he was regarded as one "who carried out rituals for those in the city in order to save them from the poison of every male and female viper and every kind of snake. . ." Another statue of Djed-hor in Cairo, which was commissioned later than the Chicago statue base, indicates that he acquired semi-divine status as a reciter of magical healing spells. It is likely that the statue that once stood on top of this base, like the Cairo statue, was covered with magical texts. Water would have been poured over the statue, magically absorbing the protective power of the spells. The liquid was then drunk as a cure for afflictions (see no. 53).

101

The texts also relate much about his career caring for the sacred falcons in the temple at Athribis. During the Late Period, animals sacred to a particular god were raised by priests of that deity. The animals were mummified and sold to pilgrims who dedicated them to the god as a sign of their piety (see no. 47). The payment (in kind) from the pilgrims provided upkeep for the temple and its staff.

The texts on the front and back of the statue base of Djed-hor recount that he "served in the service of the falcon for many years" and that he helped both in the care of the living animals and in the preparation of the mummies. He boasts that he was responsible for building a new embalming house at Athribis complete with a garden with sweet-smelling trees (perhaps a necessary antidote to the falcon yards), and a deep well "whose depth was as far as Nun" (the primordial waters). He also comments that he corrected certain irregularities in the mummification procedures: "Falcons had been found in the chamber of seventy [one of the side rooms of the catacombs?] which had not been embalmed. I caused them to be embalmed with *merhet* oil. (Then) I caused them to rest in the necropolis." He also comments that "I prepared their (falcon) burials in the necropolis. . . hidden there from foreigners," suggesting that prior to the conquest of Egypt by Alexander the Great, the Egyptians felt that they had to hide the sacred mummies from the Persian invaders.

For translation, see Sherman 1981, pp. 90–1, in Appendix 3.

53.

HORUS ON THE CROCODILES

Ptolemaic Period, 4th century B.C.

Steatite

H: 5 ¹/₂; W: 2 ³/₈; D (base): 1 ⁵/₈ in

(14.2 x 6.2 x 4.7 cm)

OIM 16881

THIS HEAVILY DECORATED statue-stela was thought to magically cure, or to afford protection from, the sting and bite of evil animals and to generally ward off evil influence. The stela, also known as a "cippus of Horus," is carved with a figure of the god Horus, his youth and vigor indicated by nudity, the immature fleshiness of his body, and the side lock usually worn by children. His power is demonstrated by his domination of evil animals—he stands on the back of crocodiles and he holds serpents, scorpions, a lion, and an oryx in his hands. The head of the protective god Bes appears above Horus. The background is carved with images of protective deities. Isis hiding her son Horus in the marshes of Chemmis and Neith with crocodiles at her sides appear to the upper right and left. Horus in his ithyphallic falcon-form, likewise standing on evil animals, is at each shoulder. The entire composition is framed by slender papyrus and lotus columns with emblems of Horus (left) and Nofertum (right). The center of the base is decorated with other, more abbreviated, images of Horus.

The sides, back, and underside of the stela are covered with finely incised hieroglyphic spells that call upon deities to protect against evil. The text begins: "Oh old one who rejuvenates himself in his time, Oh, old one who makes youth! May you cause Thoth to come to me at my voice." The text is a reference to the myth that Horus, who died from the sting of scorpions, was revived by the power of Thoth. After his revivification, he became the protector of others from such a fate. Water poured over the inscribed surfaces of the cippus was thought to absorb the potency of the prayer and the protective power of the deities. The water was drunk by the afflicted to effect magical protection.

Cippi were most popular in the Late Period. Some, whose lower edges were not decorated, were apparently socketed into bases carved with a receptacle to collect the protective water in the way that the Cairo statue of Djed-hor was mounted on a basin.

For translation, see Seele 1947, pp. 47–48, in Appendix 3.

54.
CULT STATUE OF QUEEN ARSINOE II

Ptolemaic Period, reign of
Ptolemy II, 284–246 B.C.
Basalt
L: 21 ³/₈; W: 13 ¼; H: 4 ⅓ in
(55 x 33.7 x 11 cm)
OIM 10518

THE PTOLEMAIC KINGS WHO ruled Egypt after its conquest by Alexander the Great in 332 B.C. were of Greek origin. These foreign kings adopted many Egyptian religious, artistic, and cultural customs as a way of legitimizing their rule over the native population. This fragment of a statue of Queen Arsinoe II is a relic of the state-sponsored cult of the deified Greek queen. The posthumous deification of Arsinoe II was proclaimed by her brother-husband Ptolemy II in 270 B.C., and, according to a royal decree, statues of the deified queen were placed in both Egyptian and Greek temples throughout the country. The temples and priesthood of the deified queen were supported by taxes levied upon gardens and orchards, and several cities, as well as an entire administrative province of Egypt, were named in her honor. The popularity of the cult set a precedent for the later establishment of a cult of the royal rulers in Egyptian temples.

The front surface of this statue base is inscribed in Greek with her divine name "Arsinoe Philadelphos" (Arsinoe, the Brother-Loving [Goddess]), while the top of the base is covered with her titulary and epithets written in Egyptian hieroglyphs. It is one of the few examples of a statue base inscribed in both languages. This bilingual labeling ensured that the identity of the statue was known to both Greeks and Egyptians. The lengthy text that appears in hieroglyphs was not translated into

Greek because, as suggested by a reference to the Karnak Temple, the statue may have been placed in a Theban temple that would have been visited primarily by the native population. The epithets "beloved of the god Re" and "daughter of Amun" were traditionally Egyptian, and they would have appealed to the local population. A unique feature of this inscription is her epithet "the wise," which may indicate that Arsinoe was literate.

Inscription:

The great soul, daughter of Amun, god's wife, sister of the King of Upper and Lower Egypt, Lord of the Two Lands, User-ka-re-mery-amun, daughter of Amun, Arsinoe. The great benefactor, beloved of Re, wife of the king, son of Re, lord of Appearances Ptolemy, daughter of Amun, Arsinoe. The lady, beloved of Ptah, royal sister of the King of Upper and Lower Egypt, Lord of the Two Lands, User-ka-re-mery-amun, daughter of Amun, Arsinoe the wise, beloved of Thoth, royal daughter of the Lord of the Two lands Setep-en-re- mery-amun, Lord of Appearances, Ptolemy (I), daughter of Amun Arsinoe, beloved of Amun-Re, Lord of the Thrones of the Two Lands, the foremost of Karnak, beloved of Mut the great, Mistress of Isheru, and beloved of Khonsu in Thebes, Nefer-hotep.

55.
WATER CLOCK (Clepsydra)
Ptolemaic Period, reign of Ptolemy
II, 284–246 B.C.
Limestone, carnelian beads
H: 20 ½; D (top): 26 ¼ in
(52.5 x 67 cm)
OIM 16875

THE EGYPTIANS CAREFULLY recorded time for state, economic, agricultural, and sacred functions. For much of Egyptian history, most events were tied to the civil calendar that was made up of three seasons of four months each. Each month had thirty days, with five additional days added to the calendar to equal the 365 days of the earth's rotation about the sun.

Time was measured by observation of the sun and stars, and also with measuring devices like this water clock—a vessel that equated a volume of water with a specific length of time—much as an hourglass measures time with sand. The earliest reference to a water clock is in a biographical text of the courtier Amunemhet who claimed that he made one for King Amunhotep I (ca. 1526 B.C.). The oldest surviving example (now in Cairo), dates to the reign of Amunhotep III, some 200 years later. Water clocks continued to be used in the Far East into recent times.

The exterior of this water clock is decorated with twelve panels, each representing a month of the calendar. The first month of inundation and three of the four months of summer are explicitly labeled, while the other months of the year are identified only by the deities associated with each month. A large figure of a seated baboon representing the god Thoth, the reckoner of time, sits at the front. The gods and months clockwise from the Thoth are: Tehy (month 1 of inundation); Ptah (month 2 of inundation); Hathor (month 3 of inundation); Sekhmet (month 4 of inundation); Mut (month 1 of winter); Min-Kamutef (month 2 of winter), Ta-weret (month 3 of winter); Renenutet (month 4 of winter); Khonsu (month 1 of summer); Sekhmet

(month 2 of summer); Ipet (month 3 of summer); and Re-Horakhty (month 4 of summer). The second month of winter is usually personified by a hippo-type creature or by a jackal, rather than by Sekhmet.

The interior of the water clock is drilled with holes against which the water level was measured. These holes are arranged in twelve vertical rows separated by large *ankh* or *djed* hieroglyphs. Twelve separate calibrations were necessary because the length of the night, and hence each hour, was shorter in the summer months than in the winter.

Some water clocks worked on an outflow system in which the water flowed from the container, while others measured the level of water as it entered the container at a specified rate. Since the uppermost hole in each row is at approximately the same level from the rim, and the holes stop about two thirds from the bottom of the vessel, this clock must have worked on an outflow system. However, this water clock lacks any sort of drain hole, suggesting that it was never finished. The brief hieroglyphic text for the second month of inundation suggests that this clock was a cult object, perhaps a votive, non-functioning clepsydra used in the cult of the deified Queen Arsinoe II (see no. 54).

56.

RELIEF FRAGMENT

Ptolemaic Period,

4th–1st centuries B.C.

Limestone

H: 15 ³/₄; W: 16 ⁵/₈ in (40.7 x 43 cm)

OIM 19517

THIS RELIEF OF A WOMAN exhibits the characteristic artistic style of the Ptolemaic Period. Among the most obvious features are the firm round breast placed very high on the chest and the small pursed lips. The woman is shown wearing a heavy wig with curls represented as rounded half-cylinders that fall upon her brow and in front and back of her right shoulder. She wears armlets and a beaded collar banded with tear-drop shaped beads. The straps on her V-neck dress would have been indicated in paint. She wears a headdress in the form of a vulture, the wings of which reach her shoulders. This cap, which was associated with Nekhbet, a goddess in the form of a vulture, is known from the Old Kingdom (ca. 2500 B.C.), at which time it was worn by queens and goddesses. In the New Kingdom and Late Period (ca. 1550–332 B.C.), it is shown in a wider variety of contexts. It was worn by princesses who served as priestesses (see no. 40), and it also was shown on coffins of elite women (see no. 38), where it alluded to the deceased's association with the gods. In the Ptolemaic Period (4th century B.C.–1st century A.D.), princesses no longer occupied the highest priestly offices, and the vulture crown was again restricted to queens and goddesses. Since the context of this fragment is unknown, the identity of the woman—whether she is a queen or a goddess—cannot be determined.

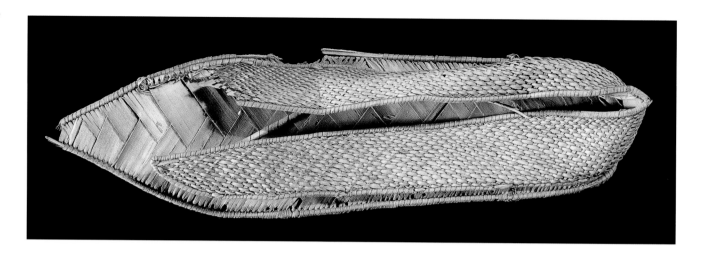

57.

SANDAL

Ptolemaic-Roman Periods,
2nd century B.C.–2nd century A.D.
Palm fiber (?)
L: 13; W: 3 ³/₈ in (33.4 x 8.75 cm)
OIM 7189

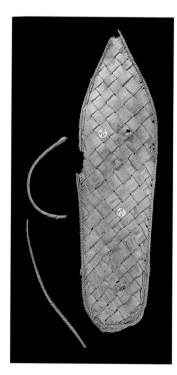

ALTHOUGH MANY PAINTINGS and reliefs depict people barefoot, texts, representations, and archaeological evidence from the earliest times indicate that Egyptians would, at least on occasion, wear some sort of foot covering. Throughout most of the pharaonic period, Egyptians wore an open sandal, most examples of which consist of a woven sole with a strap that passed over the instep and a thong that passed between the first and second toes. Some tomb paintings depict another strap around the ankle. Most examples of sandals are made of woven palm or other rush material, although some examples are made of wood or leather and ceremonial or funerary sandals made of gold and silver are also known.

Shoes and more elaborate sandals appear in the Late Period and Ptolemaic eras (7th–1st century. B.C.). This example of a sandal that nearly encloses the foot is made of three parts. The sole is plaited of broad strips of fiber. A slender bundle of long fibers has been sewn around the edge as reinforcement and decoration. The upper part of the sandal is made of a 1 ¹/₄ inch wide by approximately 21 inch long strip that surrounded and enclosed the foot except for the top surface of the toes. The strip is made of two layers of reeds. The inner facing was made of the same type of reeds and with the same plaiting technique as the sole. This was covered with a woven layer of finer, narrow fibers to produce a decorative outer surface. The layers were joined by sewing several fibers along their edges. The strip was then attached to the sole by thin fibers sewn through pairs of holes spaced along the sole. The third element of the sandal—two thongs that passed between the first and second toes—is made of coils of fiber.

The distance from the heel to the thong emplacement indicates that the sandal is the equivalent of a man's 5 or 5 ¹/₂ or a woman's size 7 or 7 ¹/₂ (American). It was for the right foot. Approximately three inches of the front of the sandal extended beyond the toes. Although today the sole is flat, representations of shoes from the Roman era suggest that the toe was probably curled upward (see no. 40).

The technique used for plaiting the sole and inner facing of this shoe is characteristic of the Ptolemaic and Roman Periods. Rush work sandals from earlier periods are generally made of rows of basketwork rather than of plaited reeds.

58.

MUMMY MASK

Roman Period, 1st century B.C.–
early 2nd century A.D.

Cartonnage, linen, pigment, gilt

H: 15 ½; W: 9 ¾; D: 10 ⅛ in
(40 x 25 x 24 cm)

OIM 7177

IN THE PTOLEMAIC and early Roman Periods (4th century B.C.–3rd century A.D.), a standard part of funerary equipment for the elite was a mask that covered the head and shoulders of the mummy. Although the faces on these masks are highly stylized and do not resemble any specific individual, they were thought to immortalize the deceased and to ensure eternal existence in the afterlife. A major concern of ancient funerary beliefs was that the mummy might decay, for it was believed that the body had to remain intact for the deceased to function in the afterlife. Preservation was also associated with the ability of an aspect of the soul called the *ba*, which was thought to leave the mummy during the daytime, only to return to its recognizable body at nightfall. The representation of eyes, nose, mouth, and ears on the mask provided imperishable and functional substitutes for those facial features. The mask also symbolized the deceased's assimilation to the gods in the afterlife.

This mask appeals to all of these functions. An image of the soul of the deceased appears on top of the mask, symbolizing its unification with the mummy. Usually represented as a human-headed bird, here it is shown as a head emerging from the body of a winged scarab—the symbol of the sun that was born anew each morning—an allusion to eternal rebirth and life. The association of the deceased with the gods is indicated by the liberal use of gold leaf on the face—a reference to the belief that the gods had skin of gold. The small pendent on the neck, in the form of the hieroglyph for the human heart, refers to the weighing of the heart at the judgment by the gods (see no. 51). In the Graeco-Roman Period, men were thought to be associated with Osiris, while women were more commonly assimilated to Hathor. The images of Osiris on a funerary shrine that appear on either side of the face suggest that this mask was made for a man.

59.
**FUNERARY STELA OF
PA-SHER-O-PEHTY**
Early Roman Period, 1st century
B.C.–1st century A.D.
Sandstone
H: 12 ⅛; W: 10 ⅛; D: 2 ⅓ in
(31 x 26 x 6 cm)
OIM 5116

THE PTOLEMAIC AND ROMAN ERA tombs at Dendera consist of a series of small, nearly square rock-cut tombs. Mummies were placed in niches cut into the tomb walls, and stelae, like this one, were placed under the head of each mummy. A common theme of the funerary stelae from Dendera was a traditional scene of Anubis, the jackal-headed god of embalming, preparing a mummy that lies on a bier with a lion head, legs, and tail. The goddesses Nephthys (right) and Isis (left) raise their hands in an attitude of mourning. Their presence and actions are symbolic of the association of the deceased with the god Osiris, who was mourned at the time of his own death by the two goddesses. The lunette of the stela is decorated with a winged disk with pendent uraei.

The Anubis and mourners motif was very common from the New Kingdom onward, attesting to the continuity of themes in religious iconography in ancient Egypt. On this example, like others from Dendera that date to the early Roman Period, the formalized liturgical hieroglyphic script which was normally employed for such stelae has been replaced by cursive demotic, the script that was then being used for ordinary purposes. The use of demotic on stone, especially on funerary stelae, is relatively rare. Not only is the highly cursive script not well suited to engraving in stone, especially coarse-grained sandstone, but during the period of this stela's manufacture most were inscribed in the traditional hieroglyphs or in Greek.

Inscription:

An offering that the king gives to Osiris, Isis, Thoth, and Anubis that they may give funerary offerings of bread, beer, oxen, and fowl, offerings and every good and pure thing to the Osiris Pa-sher-o-pehty, son of Pa-khy, his mother being Ta-khy that they may give him a good burial. May his house last forever!

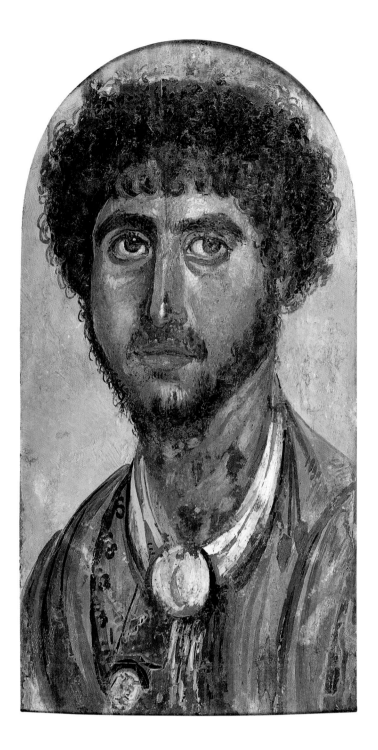

60.

MUMMY PORTRAIT

Roman Period, 2nd century A.D.

Wax (encaustic) on wood

Image H: 16 ⅛; W: 9 ⅛ in

(41.5 x 23.5 cm)

OIM 2053

SOME OF THE BEST EXAMPLES of naturalistic art from ancient Egypt are the so-called Fayum portraits, most of which date to the early and middle Roman Period (1st to the mid-3rd centuries A.D.). In these painted compositions, artists employed the western, Graeco-Roman idea of portraiture in the effort to capture the idiosyncratic features of the subject, including clothing, hairstyles, and facial hair. The use of tonal gradations and the effects of light and dark were also innovations of this style. The apparently middle-aged man shown on this example looks directly at the viewer, but his body is turned slightly away as is characteristic of such paintings. In contrast to the simple Greek-style tunic (*chiton*) that is common on such portraits, this man wears a very unusual elaborate purple tunic with a white over-cloak. The neckline of the tunic is ornamented with a white collar. The style of the tightly-curled hair and the closely-cut beard suggest a date of the 2nd century A.D.

In recent years, there has been considerable research into the question of who commissioned these portraits. For many years, it had been assumed that people of Graeco-Roman background who lived in Egypt were buried with portraits, whereas native Egyptians continued to use the traditional masks (see no. 58). However, this neat dichotomy did not take into account the social structure of the Roman Period. At the time that the portraits were being produced, Roman law no longer differentiated native Egyptians from those of Greek background, but grouped them together as non-Roman citizens in a class called *Aigyptioi*. The elite among the *Aigyptioi* had Greek names and used the Greek language, whether they were of Greek descent or not. It is known that some of these elite members of society were native Egyptians, and many of them also had Egyptian personal names. The Fayum portraits were made to appeal to this elite part of the population of Roman Egypt, who were either of Greek descent, or, through their profession, social status, and use of the Greek language, considered themselves to be of the Hellenized elite. Yet the use of the portraits in the wholly Egyptian funerary context of mummies indicates that they regarded themselves also as Egyptian.

These paintings, normally done in encaustic (melted wax) or in tempera on board, were bound over the wrapped head of a mummy. This custom is a good illustration of the permanence of traditional Egyptian funerary practices that dictated that the facial features of the deceased be duplicated, and thereby preserved to serve as functional substitutes for the vital facilities in the afterlife. Prior to the appearance of Fayum portraits, this was ensured by the face on anthropoid coffins or by cartonnage masks (see nos. 38, 58).

The style of the simple pit tombs from which most of the portrait mummies were recovered, the forms of damage suffered by the mummies, as well as demotic and Greek texts, suggest that at least some of the portrait mummies were not buried immediately after they were delivered to the family. One letter refers to the mummy of a young woman: "She has been carried to Alabanthis, so if you come and if you so wish, you can see her." It has been suggested that the mummies were displayed in tomb chapels that could be visited by family and friends, a custom that was unknown in the pharaonic period.

61.
MASK FROM A FUNERARY SHROUD

Late Roman Period,
mid-3rd century A.D.
Linen, stucco, gum, pigment
H: 10 ½; W: 13 ¼ in (26.6 x 33.6 cm)
OIM 9385

THE TRADITION OF PLACING a representation of the deceased over the face of the mummified corpse persisted well into the early Christian Period (4th century A.D.). In earlier centuries, the representations were in the form of cartonnage masks that covered the head and shoulders (see no. 58), more naturalistic "portraits" painted on board (see no. 60), plaster heads, and shrouds with painted representations. By the mid-3rd century A.D., the cartonnage masks and "portraits" were replaced by a piece of linen with a face molded in plaster in high relief. Referred to as shrouds or masks, they are a hybrid. They are longer than the old style mask, covering much of the front of the torso, but they do not cover the back of the head. More intact examples show that the torso with details of clothing was painted directly on the linen below the molded face.

This sort of shroud shows the fusion of Egyptian and Roman influences. The practice of placing a representation of the deceased upon the mummy and the references to traditional Egyptian funerary deities are traditional Egyptian conceptions. On the shrouds they are combined with clothing, hairstyle, and jewelry that were introduced into Egypt from Rome. On this example, the woman wears her hair in curls around her face, exposing her ears, a style that is well attested for the 3rd and 4th centuries. She wears a floral diadem, a ubiquitous feature of these masks, which is thought to symbolize the transfiguration of the deceased. Her Roman-style earrings are painted in imitation of gold and pearls, and a rich necklace of alternating colored gems, each framed in gold, is painted on the neck of her tunic.

62.

LAMP IN THE FORM OF A BIRD
Byzantine Period,
6th–8th centuries A.D.
Bronze
H: 4; L: 4; W: 2 ⅓ in
(10.5 x 10.5 x 5.85 cm).
Length of chain: 5 in (12.7 cm).
OIM 16734

WITH THE CONVERSION of Egypt to Christianity in the early centuries A.D., artists gradually adopted new decorative themes, such as peacocks, doves, and crosses, which were associated with the new religion. This oil lamp is fashioned in the form of a bird—most probably a peacock or a dove. Lamps in the form of a dove—a symbol of the Holy Ghost—were perhaps a pun, for the Holy Ghost enlightened mankind just as the lamp would bring light to its owner. The tail of this lamp forks into two spouts which held wicks, one of which is still in place. The spouts are inscribed "Mary" and "One God" in Greek. A triangular opening in the back of the bird allowed oil to be poured into the lamp. The opening was once covered by a small bronze lid hinged to the bird's back. The small loops (one is now missing) at the leading and trailing edges of each wing may have been points for anchoring the lamp to prevent it from swaying.

The bird is detailed with markings that imitate individual feathers. Its eyes are indicated by small circles. A ring-like collar is shown around its neck. A loop on its chest holds a small circle of wire. Pierced ear tufts are shown on either side of its head—one of which still holds a curl of wire. A small protrusion of metal allowed for the attachment of the bird's head crest. The upper surface of the beak is highly curved. Although the lamp was hung by the chain that is attached at three points of its body, a support behind the feet and a platform that connect the splayed feet allowed the lamp to stand.

The lamp was excavated from the ruins of a Coptic church near the palace of the temple of Aye at Medinet Habu (Luxor). This region in southern Egypt was home to many Coptic monasteries—four were located at Medinet Habu alone—and others were built in the desert to the west of the ruins of the pharaonic temple.

GLOSSARY

Akh An element of the human soul that underwent transfiguration to a blessed status upon rebirth.

Amulet Good luck/protective charm, often in the form of a hieroglyph.

Ankh Hieroglyph in the form of a cross with a looped top meaning "to live" and "life."

Apis bull Bull sacred to the god Ptah and later to the god Osiris-Serapis.

Archaic Period Synonym for Early Dynastic Period, or Dynasties 1 and 2.

Atum Primeval cosmic creator god who was associated with the setting sun.

Ba An element of the soul of the deceased that was thought to be able to leave the tomb and to maintain contact with the realm of the living; shown in the form of a human-headed bird.

Barque A boat; often a sacred boat used to transport a statue of a god or the king.

Book of the Dead Modern name for a series of New Kingdom and later religious texts intended to protect the soul of the deceased as it traveled through the under-world toward rebirth. In ancient Egypt the Book of the Dead was called [The Book of] "Going Forth By Day."

Canopic jar Vessel of stone, pottery, or wood in which mummified organs were stored in the tomb. Burials were equipped with four canopic jars, one each for the stomach, liver, lungs, and intestines which were removed during the mummification process. "Canopic" refers to the Classical Period god Canopus who was represented in a form that resembled a jar for the viscera.

Cartonnage Papier-mâché-like material made of layers of papyrus, gum, fabric, and plaster, used to make anthropoid coffins and other fittings for mummies.

Cartouche Representation of an oval-shaped loop of rope that encircles a royal name, derived from the *shen* (see below). It symbolizes that the king ruled all that the sun enclosed.

Cataract Outcroppings of rock in the Nile that created rapids which made river travel difficult. The six cataracts from near Khartoum to Aswan protected Egypt from invasion from the south.

Cenotaph Symbolic tomb.

Cippus (pl. cippi) Statue or amulet inscribed with religious texts that was thought to have medicinal power. The most common form in Egypt is the cippus of Horus decorated with a figure of the youthful Horus. Cippi are usually inscribed with texts that call upon Isis, the mother of Horus, to cure afflictions.

Coptic Branch of Christianity prevalent in Egypt; from the Greek *aiguptios* for "Egypt," also the last stage of the ancient Egyptian language, written primarily in Greek letters.

Demotic Late stage of Egyptian language and also the cursive script used to write it from about 650 B.C. to the 5th century A.D.

Djed pillar Hieroglyph in the form of a column with horizontal lines across its upper section, thought to represent the backbone of the god Osiris. It was the phonogram for "stability." Amulets and representations of *djed* columns are frequently associated with mummies and funerary objects.

Double crown A composite crown composed of a nested white crown of Upper Egypt and the red crown of Lower Egypt. It symbolized the king's rule over all of Egypt.

Dynasty A series of rulers, often from the same line of descent; generally traced from father to son.

Eye of Horus see *wedjat*

Faience Quartz paste-based material that was molded and fired. It was used to make statuettes, amulets, and ritual vessels. Often bright blue or blue green, it could be glazed in a variety of colors.

False beard Beard attached to the chin with straps. The false beard worn by the king was straight and rectangular, while that worn by Osiris and other deities, as well as the deceased associated with Osiris, was slender, curved, and plaited.

False door Architectural feature of tombs and temples; representation of a door. In temples, it functioned as the focus of cult activities. In a tomb it was the portal through which the soul passed between the tomb chamber and the burial shaft, and it was also the place where food offerings for the deceased were placed.

Feast of the Valley Annual festival celebrated in ancient Luxor in which the sacred barques of the gods and the king visited tombs and royal funerary temples on the west bank of the Nile.

God's Father Clerical title which, from the Old Kingdom to the early New Kingdom, was applied to a relative of the king (who was referred to as "god"). By the New Kingdom, God's Father became a more general priestly title without reference to a relationship to the king.

Hieratic Cursive form of hieroglyphs commonly used for record-keeping, correspondence, and some religious texts.

Ka One of the elements of the soul, represented in human form. It was the aspect of the soul that needed food and provisions after death. The symbol of the *ka* is two uplifted arms.

Karnak Temple Complex of temples at modern Luxor, dominated by the Temple of Amun, but also including temples to Mut, Khonsu, Montu, and Ipet.

Lower Egypt Northern Egypt, approximately from the apex of the Delta just south of today's Cairo northward to the shore of the Mediterranean. The designation "Lower" refers to the southward flow of the Nile.

Maat Truth, justice, righteousness; also the goddess (Maat) who is the embodiment of truth and universal order.

Mastaba Mud brick or stone rectangular tomb superstructure characteristic of Early Dynastic royal tombs and private tombs of the Old and Middle Kingdoms.

Naos A shrine, usually in the sanctuary of the temple, in which a cult statue of the god resided.

Natron Desiccating agent (sodium carbonate and bicarbonate) used in the preparation of mummies. Large deposits of natron occur in the Wadi Natrun northwest of Cairo.

Nemes Blue and yellow-striped fabric head cover worn by the king.

Nilometer Staircase or stone surface marked with calibrations to record the height of the Nile flood.

Nome Greek name for administrative districts of Egypt.

Nomen The equivalent of the personal name of the king born by him or her prior to accession to the throne.

Nubia Area between the First and Sixth Nile cataracts (today's southern Egypt and northern Sudan).

Osiris Major deity of the afterlife; from the Old Kingdom onward the deceased was associated with Osiris.

Ostracon (pl. ostraca) Flake of limestone or piece of pottery used for written records or for sketching.

Papyrus Paper-like substance made of overlapped strips of the papyrus stalk.

Pharaoh Title for the king of Egypt attested from the New Kingdom onward; from Egyptian *per-aa* meaning "great house," a reference to the residence of the king.

Phyle Administrative term for a division of temple priests.

Prenomen The coronation name of the king. The prenomen is normally compounded with the name of the sun god Re.

Pyramid Texts Religious texts incised on the walls of pyramid burial chambers from Dynasties 5 to 12 intended to protect the spirit of the king in the afterlife.

Raised relief Technique of carving on stone wherein the background is cut away, leaving the scene standing above the background. Also known as bas relief.

Scarab A beetle (*Scarabaeus sacer*); the hieroglyph for "to come into being" or "to exist," hence its use as an amulet of rejuvenation.

Serdab Statue chamber in an Old Kingdom tomb.

Shabti (also spelled ushebti, shawabti) see Ushebti

Shen Circular hieroglyph representing a loop of rope, meaning "circuit [of the sun]," and by extension "eternity."

Sistrum (pl. sistra) Ritual rattle, most commonly associated with the goddess Hathor.

Stela (pl. stelae) Surface of stone or wood carved or painted with scenes or texts; often a monument to the dead or the record of a historical event.

Sunk relief Technique of carving on stone wherein the design is cut into the stone, leaving the background standing above it.

Titulary Series of names and epithets of the king that praised him and associated him with deities.

Upper Egypt Southern and central Egypt from Aswan north to the area just south of today's Cairo. The designation "Upper" refers to the southward flow of the Nile.

Uraeus (pl. uraei) Protective ornament in the form of a cobra that appears on the forehead of kings, queens, and deities. Texts relate that the cobra spit protective fire.

Ushebti Mummiform statuette deposited in tombs from Dynasty 13 onward to act as a servant for the deceased.

Valley of the Kings Valley on the west bank of Luxor containing tombs of New Kingdom kings and a few noblemen.

Valley of the Queens Valley on the west bank of Luxor containing tombs of New Kingdom queens, princes, and nobility.

Vizier A position in the Egyptian bureaucracy similar to that of a modern prime minister. The vizier acted as chief advisor, head of administration, and supreme judge.

Vulture headdress/crown Headdress in the form of a bird, the wings of which cover each side of the head, with the vulture head at the wearer's forehead. The vulture cap was worn by queens and by goddesses and is also shown on coffins of elite women.

Was scepter A hieroglyph in the form of a tall slender staff with a forked bottom and a recurved top in the form of an animal head with tall ears, somewhat like a stylized jackal. *Was* means "dominion."

Wedjat eye (also spelled udjat) A human eye and eyebrow combined with the stylized markings of a falcon eye, representing the eye of the falcon-god Horus. The *wedjat* means to "be whole" or "healthy" through the myth that the eye of Horus was plucked out by the evil god Seth and was later restored by Thoth. The eye was associated with the moon, the waxing of which was equated with regeneration.

BIBLIOGRAPHY OF WORKS CONSULTED

Andrews, Carol. *Amulets of Ancient Egypt.* London: The British Museum Press, 1994.

Armitage, P. L. and J. Clutton-Brock. "Radiological and Histological Investigation into Mummification of Cats." *Journal of Archaeological Science* 8 (1981): 185–96.

Arnold, Dieter. *Temples of the Last Pharaohs.* New York: Oxford University Press, 1999.

Arnold, Dorothea and Christiane Ziegler (editors). *Egyptian Art in the Age of the Pyramids.* New York: Metropolitan Museum of Art, 1999.

Assmann, Jan. *Grabung im Asasif 1963–1970.* Vol. 2. *Das Grab des Basa (nr. 389) in der thebanischen Nekropole.* Archäologische Veröffentlichungen, Deutsches Archäologisches Institut Kairo 6. Mainz: Philipp von Zabern, 1973.

Badaway, Alexander. *Coptic Art and Archaeology: The Art of the Christian Egyptians from the Late Antique to the Middle Ages.* Cambridge: MIT Press, 1978.

Bagnall, Roger. "The People of the Roman Fayum." In *Portraits and Masks: Burial Customs in Roman Egypt,* edited by Morris Bierbriar, pp. 7–15. London: The British Museum Press, 1997.

von Beckerath, Jürgen. *Chronologie des pharaonischen Ägypten.* Mainz: Philipp von Zabern.

Bénazeth, Dominique. *L'art du métal du début de l'ère chrétienne.* Musée du Louvre, Catalogue du Département des Antiquités Égyptiennes. Paris: Réunion des musées nationaux, 1992.

Bierbrier, Morris. *The Late New Kingdom in Egypt (1300–664 B.C.): A Genealogical and Chronological Investigation.* Warminster: Aris and Phillips, 1975.

Bothmer, Bernard. *Egyptian Sculpture of the Late Period 700 B.C. to A.D. 100.* Brooklyn: The Brooklyn Museum, 1960.

Breasted, Charles. *Pioneer to the Past: The Story of James Henry Breasted, Archaeologist.* New York: Charles Scribner's Sons, 1947.

Breasted, James H. *The Oriental Institute.* The University of Chicago Survey 12. Chicago: The University of Chicago Press, 1933.

Brooklyn Museum. *Pagan and Christian Egypt: Egyptian Art from the First to the Tenth Century A.D.* Brooklyn: The Brooklyn Museum Press, 1941.

————. *Late Egyptian and Coptic Art.* Brooklyn: The Brooklyn Museum Press, 1943.

————. *Cleopatra's Egypt: The Age of the Ptolemies.* Brooklyn: The Brooklyn Museum Press, 1988.

Brovarski, Edward, Susan Doll, and Rita Freed (editors). *Egypt's Golden Age: The Art of Living in the New Kingdom 1558–1085 B.C.* Boston: Museum of Fine Arts, 1982.

Brunner-Traut, Emma and Helmut Brunner. *Die ägyptische Sammlung der Universität Tübingen.* Mainz: Philipp von Zabern, 1981.

————. *Osiris, Kreuz und Halbmond. Die drei Religionen Ägyptens.* Mainz: Philipp von Zabern, 1984.

Cooney, John. *Five Years of Collecting Egyptian Art 1951–1956.* Brooklyn: The Brooklyn Museum Press, 1956.

Cotterell, Brian and Johan Kamminga. *Mechanics of Pre-Industrial Technology.* Cambridge: Cambridge University Press, 1990.

D'Auria, Sue, Peter Lacovara, and Catherine Roehrig (editors). *Mummies and Magic.* Boston: Museum of Fine Arts, 1988.

Dodson, Aiden. "Canopic Jars and Chests." In *The Oxford Encyclopedia of Ancient Egypt,* edited by Donald B. Redford, Vol. 1, pp. 231–35. Oxford: Oxford University Press, 2001.

Doxiadis, Euphrosyne. *The Mysterious Fayum Portraits.* New York: Abrams, 1995.

Faulkner, Raymond O. *The Ancient Egyptian Pyramid Texts.* Oxford: The Clarendon Press, 1969.

Fischer, Henry. *Denderah in the Third Millennium B.C.* Locust Valley (NY): J. J. Augustin, 1968.

————. *Varia Nova.* Egyptian Studies III. New York: The Metropolitan Museum of Art, 1996.

Fosdick, Raymond B. *John D. Rockefeller, Jr.: A Portrait.* New York: Harper, 1956.

Friedman, Florence D. *Beyond the Pharaohs: Egypt and the Copts in the 2nd to 7th centuries* A.D. Providence: Rhode Island School of Design, 1989.

Gaballa, Gaballa Ali. "False Door Stelae of Some Memphite Personnel." *Studien zur altägyptischen Kultur* 7 (1979): 41–52

Gardiner, Alan H. *Ancient Egyptian Onomastica.* Vol. 2. London: Oxford University Press, 1947.

Gardiner, Alan H. and Kurt Sethe. *Egyptian Letters to the Dead Mainly from the Old and Middle Kingdoms.* London: The Egypt Exploration Society, 1928.

Graefe, Erhart. Das Ritualgerät *šbt/wnšb/wt t.*" In *Studien zu Sprache und Religion Ägyptens,* edited by F. Junge, pp. 895–905. Göttingen: Hubert and Co., 1984.

Green, Christine. *The Temple Furniture from the Sacred Animal Necropolis at North Saqqara 1964–1976.* London: The Egypt Exploration Society, 1987.

Grzimek, Bernard (editor). *Grzimek's Animal Life Encyclopedia.* Vol. 4. *Fishes I.* New York: Van Nostrand Reinhold Co., 1972–1975.

Hayes, William. *Glazed Tiles from a Palace of Ramesses II at Kantir.* New York: The Metropolitan Museum of Art, 1937.

Höltzl, Regina. "Round Topped Stelae from the Middle Kingdom to the Late Period: Some Remarks on the Decoration of the Lunettes." In *Atti VI Congresso Internazionale di Egittologia,* Vol. 1, pp. 285–89. Turin: 1992.

Hornung, Erik. *Conceptions of God in Ancient Egypt: The One and the Many.* Ithaca: Cornell University Press, 1982.

Houlihan, Patrick. *The Animal World of the Pharaohs.* New York: Thames and Hudson, 1996.

Johnson, Janet. "The Legal Status of Women in Ancient Egypt." In *Mistress of the House, Mistress of Heaven,* edited by Anne K. Capel and Glenn Markoe, pp. 175–86; 215–17. New York: Hudson Hills Press, 1996.

_____. "Speculations on Middle Kingdom Marriage." In *Studies on Ancient Egypt in Honour of H. Smith,* edited by Anthony Leahy and John Tait, pp. 169–72. London: The Egypt Exploration Society, 1999.

Jørgensen, Mogens. *Egypt I.* Catalogue/Ny Carlsberg Glyptotek. Copenhagen: Ny Carlsberg Glyptotek, 1996.

Junge, F. "Saitische Formel." In *Lexikon der Ägyptologie,* edited by Wolfgang Helck, Vol. V, cols. 357–58. Wiesbaden: Otto Harrassowitz, 1984.

Kanawati, Naguib. "The Reading of the Name Ḥrwj/ʿntjwj/Nmtjwj/B3wj." *Göttinger Miszellen* 87 (1985): 39–44.

Kemp, Barry. "The Osiris Temple at Abydos." *Mitteilungen des Deutschen Archäologischen Instituts, Abteilung Kairo* 23 (1967): 138–55.

Kozloff, Arielle, Betsy Bryan, and Lawrence Berman (editors). *Egypt's Dazzling Sun: Amenhotep and his World.* Cleveland: Cleveland Museum of Art, 1992.

Lacau, Pierre. *Catalogue Général des Antiquités Égyptiennes du Musée du Caire: Stèles du Nouvel Empire CGC 34001–34064.* Cairo: Institut français d'archéologie orientale du Caire, 1909.

Leprohon, Ronald J. *Corpus Antiquitatum Aegyptiacarum.* Fascicle 3. *Stelae II: Museum of Fine Arts, Boston.* Mainz/Rhein: Philipp von Zabern, 1985.

Lucas, Alfred. *Ancient Egyptian Materials and Industries.* Second edition. London: Edward Arnold, 1934.

Lüddeckens, Erich. "Untersuchungen über Religiösen Gehalt, Sprache und Form der ägyptischen Totenklagen." *Mitteilungen des Deutschen Archäologischen Instituts, Abteilung Kairo* 11 (1943): 1–188.

Malek, Jaromir. *The Cat in Ancient Egypt.* London: The British Museum Press, 1993.

Mariette, Auguste. *Les Mastabas de l'Ancien Empire*. 1899. Reprint, Hildesheim and New York: Georg Olms, 1976.

Montserrat, Dominic. "Death and Funerals in the Roman Fayum." In *Portraits and Masks: Burial Customs in Roman Egypt*, edited by Morris Bierbrier, pp. 33–44. London: The British Museum Press, 1997.

Montserrat, Dominic and Lynn Meskell. "Mortuary Archaeology and Religious Landscape at Graeco-Roman Deir el-Medina." *Journal of Egyptian Archaeology* 83 (1997): 179–97.

Mostafa, Doha. "A propos d'une particularité dans la décoration des tympans des stèles cintrées du Nouvel Empire." *Göttinger Miszellen* 133 (1993): 85–96.

Moussa, Ahmed and Hartwig Altenmüller. *Das Grab des Nianchchnum und Chnumhotep*. Archäologische Veröffentlichung, Deutsches Archäologisches Institut Kairo 21. Mainz: Philipp von Zabern, 1977.

Murnane, William. *Texts from the Amarna Period in Egypt*. Atlanta: Scholar's Press, 1995.

Nord, Del. "The Term ḫnr: 'harem' or 'musical performers'?" In *Studies in Ancient Egypt, the Aegean, and the Sudan*, edited by William K. Simpson and Whitney M. Davis, pp. 137–48. Boston: Museum of Fine Arts, 1981.

O'Connor, David. "The 'Cenotaphs' of the Middle Kingdom at Abydos." In *Mélanges Gamal Eddin Mokhtar*, edited by Paule Posener-Kriéger, Vol. 2, pp. 161–77. Bibliothèque d'Études 97/2. Cairo: Institut français d'archéologie orientale du Caire, 1985.

Parker, Richard. *Ancient Egyptian Calendars*. Studies in Ancient Oriental Civilization 60. Chicago: The University of Chicago Press, 1950.

Parkinson, Richard. *Cracking Codes: The Rosetta Stone and Decipherment*. Berkeley: University of California Press, 1999.

Peck, William and John Ross. *Egyptian Drawings*. New York: E. P. Dutton, 1978.

Petrie, W. M. Flinders. *Abydos, Part I, 1902*. Egypt Exploration Fund Twenty-second Memoir. London: The Egypt Exploration Fund, 1902.

———. *Hyksos and Israelite Cities*. 1906. Reprint, London: Histories and Mysteries of Man Ltd., 1989.

———. *Roman Portraits and Memphis*. British School of Archaeology in Egypt Memoir 20. London: University College, 1911.

———. *The Royal Tombs of the First Dynasty 1900, Part I*. Egypt Exploration Fund Eighteenth Memoir. London: The Egypt Exploration Fund, 1900.

———. *The Royal Tombs of the Earliest Dynasties 1901, Part II*. Egypt Exploration Fund Twenty-first Memoir. London: The Egypt Exploration Fund, 1901.

Petrie, W. M. Flinders., G. A. Wainwright, and A. H. Gardiner. *Tarkhan I and Memphis V*. British School of Archaeology in Egypt and The Egyptian Research Account. London: School of Archaeology in Egypt/Bernard Quaritch, 1913.

Piankoff, Alexandre. *The Pyramid of Unis*. Bollingen Series XL.5. Princeton: Princeton University Press, 1968.

Pinch, Geraldine. *Magic in Ancient Egypt*. London: The British Museum, 1994.

———. *Votive Offerings for Hathor*. Oxford: The Griffith Institute, 1993.

Pogo, Alexander. "Ancient Egyptian Waterclocks." *Isis* 25 (1936): 403–25.

Quibell, J. E. *The Ramesseum*. Egyptian Research Account Second Memoir. London: The Egypt Exploration Fund, 1898.

Ray, John D. *The Archive of Hor*. Texts from Excavations 2. London: The Egypt Exploration Society, 1976.

Riggs, Christina. "Facing the Dead: Recent Research on the Funerary Art of Ptolemaic and Roman Egypt." *American Journal of Archaeology* 106 (2002): 85–101.

Ritner, Robert K. "Horus on the Crocodiles: A Juncture of Religion and Magic in Late Dynastic Egypt." In *Religion and Philosophy in Ancient Egypt*, edited by William K. Simpson, pp. 103–16. Yale Egyptological Studies 3. New Haven: Yale University Press, 1989.

———. *The Mechanics of Ancient Egyptian Magical Practice*. Studies in Ancient Oriental Civilization 54. Chicago: The Oriental Institute, 1993.

Romano, James. Review of *Die Entwicklung und Bedeutung des kuboiden Statuentypus*, by Regine Schulz. *Journal of Egyptian Archaeology* 81 (1995): 250–54.

el-Saghir, Mohammed. *Statuenversteck im Luxortempel*. Mainz: Philipp von Zabern, 1992.

Saleh, Mohammed and Hourig Sourozian. *Official Catalogue of the Egyptian Museum, Cairo*. Mainz: Philipp von Zabern, 1987.

Sambin, Chantal. "Les objects *šbt* des musées." *Bulletin de l'Institut français d'archéologie orientale* 87 (1987): 275–92.

Schäfer, Heinrich. *Principles of Egyptian Art.* Oxford: Clarendon Press, 1974.

Schulz, Regine. *Die Entwicklung und Bedeutung des kuboiden Statuentypus.* Hildesheimer ägyptologische Beiträge 33–34. Hildesheim: Gerstenberg Verlag, 1992.

Settgast, Jürgen. *Untersuchungen zu altägyptischen Bestattungsdarstellungen.* Abhandlungen des Deutschen Archäologischen Instituts Kairo, Ägyptologische Reihe 3. Glückstadt/Hamburg/ New York: J. J. Augustin, 1963.

Simpson, William K. "Reshep in Egypt." *Orientalia* 29 (1960): 63–74.

————. *The Terrace of the Great God at Abydos.* Publications of the Pennsylvania-Yale Expedition to Egypt 5. New Haven and Philadelphia: Peabody Museum of Yale University and the University Museum of the University of Pennsylvania, 1974.

Sloley, R. W. "Ancient Clepsydrae." *Ancient Egypt* (June 1924): 43–50.

————. "Primitive Methods of Measuring Time." *Journal of Egyptian Archaeology* 17 (1931): 166–78.

Spallinger, Anthony. "Calendars." In *The Oxford Encyclopedia of Ancient Egypt*, edited by Donald B. Redford, Vol. 1, pp. 224–27. Oxford: Oxford University Press, 2001.

Spencer, A. Jeffrey. *Early Egypt: The Rise of Civilization in the Nile Valley.* London: British Museum Press, 1993.

Taylor, John. *Death and the Afterlife in Ancient Egypt.* Chicago: University of Chicago Press, 2001.

te Velde, Herman. *Seth, God of Confusion.* Probleme der Ägyptologie 6. Leiden: E. J. Brill, 1977.

Thompson, Dorothy. *Memphis under the Ptolemies.* Princeton: Princeton University Press, 1988.

Tooley, Angela. *Egyptian Models and Scenes.* Shire Egyptology 22. Princes Risborough: Shire, 1995.

Török, Làszló. *Coptic Antiquities.* Vol. 1. Rome: L'Ermadi Bretschneider, 1993.

Troy, Lana. *Patterns of Queenship in ancient Egyptian myth and history.* Acta Universitatis Upsallensis Boreas 14. Uppsala Studies in ancient Mediterranean and Near Eastern Civilizations. Uppsala: University of Uppsala, 1986.

Werbrouck, Marcelle. "À propos du disc ailé." *Chronique d'Égypte* 16, no. 31 (1941): 165–71.

Wild, Henri. "Contributions à l'iconographie et à la titulature de Quen-Amen." *Bulletin de l'Institut français d'archéologie orientale* 56 (1957): 203–37.

Winlock, Herbert V. *Models of Daily Life in Ancient Egypt from the Tomb of Meket-Re' at Thebes.* Publications of the Metropolitan Museum of Art, Egyptian Expedition 18. Cambridge: Harvard University Press, 1955.

Winnicki, J. K. "Demotische Stelen aus Terenuthis." In *Life in a Multi-Cultural Society: Egypt from Cambyses to Constantine and Beyond*, edited by Janet H. Johnson, pp. 351–60. Studies in Ancient Oriental Civilization 51. Chicago: The Oriental Institute, 1992.

APPENDICES

1. OBJECTS BY REGISTRATION NUMBER

2. PROVENANCE OF CATALOGUE OBJECTS

1. Votive Plaque 7911
   Abydos, grave M69, Egypt Exploration Fund, 1902–03
   Gift of the Egypt Exploration Fund, 1903

2. Mehen Game Board 16950
   Purchased in Egypt, 1932

3. Panel from the Tomb of Nefermaat and Itet 9002
   Medum, mastaba 16
   Gift of the British School of Archaeology in Egypt, 1909–10

4. False Door of Ny-su-redi 10825
   Purchased in Cairo, 1920

5. The Confectioner, Tchenenet 14054
   Purchased in London, 1933

6. Singers and Dancers 10590
   Giza (?)
   Purchased in Cairo, 1920

7. "Servant" Statues from the tomb of Ny-kau-inpu 10618, 10628, 10635, 10641, 10642,
   Giza (?), tomb of Ny-kau-inpu
   Purchased in Cairo, 1920

8. Nen-khefet-ka and his Wife Nefer-shemes 2036
   Deshasheh, tomb of Nen-khefet-ka and Nen-khef-ek
   Gift of the Egypt Exploration Fund, 1897

9. Lintel of Kha-bau-ptah 10815
   Sakkara, tomb no. 19 (Mariette no. D42)
   Purchased in Cairo, 1920

10. A Warning to Tomb Robbers 10814
    Sakkara, tomb N. IV, chapel II
    Purchased in Cairo, 1920

11. The Royal Herald, Neni 11489
    Sedment el Gebel, tomb 613
    Gift of the British School of Archaeology, 1921

12. Uha and his Wife Henut-sen 16956
    Naga ed-Deir (?)
    Purchased in Cairo, 1935

13. Model Workshop 11495
    Sedment el Gebel, tomb 2105
    Gift of the British School of Archaeology in Egypt, 1921

14. A Letter to the Dead 13945
    Purchased in Cairo, 1929

15. Stela of the Household of Senbu 6739
    Abydos, tomb E312
    Gift of the Egyptian Research Account, 1902

16. Nakht and Seth-Antewy 10510
    Purchased in Cairo, 1919

17. Funerary Figure of Kenamun 25648
    Zaweit Abu Musallam
    Gift of Mr. Eugene Chesrow, 1985

18. Child's Tunic 18285
    Luxor, Deir el Bahari
    By exchange with the Metropolitan Museum of Art, 1950

19. Statue of a God 10607
    Purchased in Luxor, 1919

20. Game of Twenty Squares 371
    Purchased in Egypt, 1894–95

21. Detail of a Funerary Procession 11047
    Luxor, Tomb of Huy (Theban tomb 54)
    Purchased in Cairo, 1920

22. Running Ibexes 11398
    Purchased from the Egyptian Museum, Cairo, 1920

23. Colossal Statue of Tutankhamun 14088
    Luxor, Medinet Habu
    Excavated by the Oriental Institute, 1930

24. Amun 10503
    Purchased in Cairo, 1919

25. Seti I and Ramesses II 10507
    Abydos (?)
    Purchased in Cairo, 1919

26. Two Scenes of Nature 16879, 16880
    Purchased in Luxor, 1933

27. The Bad Boy 13951
Purchased in Luxor, 1931

28. Stela Dedicated to the God Reshep
10569
Purchased in Cairo, 1920

29. Decorative Tiles
Luxor, Medinet Habu
16672: Excavated by the Oriental
Institute, 1928
16721: Excavated by the Oriental
Institute, 1931

30. Floral Column 14089
Luxor, Medinet Habu
Excavated by the Oriental Institute,
1931–32

31. Grooming Implements
76: Purchased in Egypt, 1984–5
8515: Oxyrhyncus
Gift of the Egypt Exploration Fund,
1904
9912: Purchased in Cairo, 1919
10502: Purchased in Cairo, 1919
10582: Purchased in Cairo, 1920

32. Study for a Royal Tomb Painting 17006
Luxor, Deir el Medina (?)
Purchased in Egypt, 1936

33. Head of a King 15554
Luxor, Medinet Habu
Excavated by the Oriental Institute

34. Canopic Jars 2091–2094
Luxor, Deir el Bahari
Gift of the Egyptian Research Account,
1897

35. A Priest of Hathor 10729
Dendera
Purchased in Egypt, 1919

36. Stela of the Hearing Ear 16718
Luxor, Medinet Habu
Excavated by the Oriental Institute,
1929

37. Offering to the God 1351
Luxor, Ramesseum
Gift of the Egypt Exploration Fund,
1896

38. Cartonnage Case and Mummy of
Meresamun 10797
Purchased in Egypt, 1919

39. Brick Stamp 11171
Purchased in Cairo, 1919

40. Amunirdis I and Diese-heb-sed 14681
Luxor, Medinet Habu
Excavated by the Oriental Institute,
1929

41. Reliefs from the Tomb of Montuemhet
17973–75, 18828
Luxor, tomb of Montuemhet (Theban
tomb 34)
17973–75: Purchased in Oakland, CA,
1948
18828: Purchased in New York, 1952

42. Statue of Amun 10584
Purchased in Egypt, 1920

43. Stela of Harsiese 12220
Gift of G. F. Maynard and Family, 1925

44. Donation Stela 13943
Purchased in Egypt, 1929

45. Composite Deity 11375
Purchased in Cairo, 1920

46. Demotic "Marriage" Papyrus 17481
Hawara
Purchased in Cairo, 1932

47. Head from a Cat Coffin 18826
Purchased in New York, 1952, partial
gift of Mr. and Mrs. Hans van der
Morwitz

48. Oracular Statue in the Form of a Falcon
10504
Purchased in Cairo, 1919

49. Thoth Emblem 10101
Purchased in Paris, 1919

50. Ritual Vessel (Situla) 11394
Purchased in Cairo, 1920

51. Book of the Dead 9787
Purchased in Paris, 1919, Gift of Martin
Ryerson

52. Statue Base of Djed-hor 10589
    Athribis
    Purchased in Egypt, 1919

53. Horus on the Crocodiles 16881
    Purchased in Egypt, 1933

54. Cult Statue of Queen Arsinoe II 10518
    Karnak?
    Purchased in Luxor, 1930

55. Water Clock (Clepsydra) 16875
    Memphis (?)
    Purchased in Egypt in 1933

56. Relief Fragment 19517
    Gift of Mrs. I. B. Soriano in memory of
    her mother, Mrs. Chauncey J. Blair,
    1962

57. Sandal 7189
    Fayum, grave H 17
    Gift of the Egypt Exploration Fund,
    1903

58. Mummy Mask 7177
    Fayum
    Gift of the Egypt Exploration Fund,
    1903

59. Funerary Stela of Pa-sher-o-pehty 5116
    Dendera
    Gift of the Egypt Exploration Fund,
    1898

60. Mummy Portrait 2053
    Hawara
    Gift of the Egypt Exploration Fund,
    1897

61. Mask from a Funerary Shroud 9385
    Deir el Bahari
    The Egypt Exploration Fund, 1897
    Gift of the Art Institute of Chicago, 1917

62. Lamp in the Form of a Bird 16734
    Luxor, Medinet Habu
    Excavated by the Oriental Institute, 1932

3. PRIOR PUBLICATION OF CATALOGUE OBJECTS

1. Votive Plaque 7911

   Kaplony, Peter. *Die Inschriften der Ägyptischen Frühzeit.* Ägyptologische Abhandlungen 8. Vol. 1. Wiesbaden: Otto Harrassowitz, 1963, p. 553.

   Petrie, W. M. Flinders. *Abydos Part II.* The Egypt Exploration Fund Memoir 22. London: The Egyptian Exploration Fund, 1903, p. 25, frontispiece, pl. 5 (33).

2. Mehen Game Board 16950

   Piccione, Peter. "Mehen Mysteries and Resurrection from the Coiled Serpent." *Journal of the American Research Center in Egypt* 27 (1990): 46–7, fig. 3.

3. Panel from the tomb of Nefermaat and Itet 9002 (selected references)

   Harpur, Yvonne. *The Tombs of Nefermaat and Rahotep at Maidum: Discovery, Destruction and Reconstruction.* Cheltenham: Oxford Expedition to Egypt, 2001, pp. 83–84, figs. 84, 169, 177, pl. 27.

   Parkinson, Richard. *Cracking Codes: The Rosetta Stone and Decipherment.* Berkeley: University of California Press, 1999, p. 138.

   Petrie, W. M. Flinders. *Medum.* London: D. Nutt, 1892, p. 26, pl. xxiv.

4. False Door of Ny-su-redi 10825
   Unpublished

5. The Confectioner, Tchenenet 14054

   Silverman, David. "An Old Kingdom Statue in the Oriental Institute Museum." *Journal of Near Eastern Studies* 32 (1973): 466–76.

6. Singers and Dancers 10590

   Vandier, Jacques. *Manuel d'archéologie Égyptienne.* Vol. 4. *Bas-reliefs et Peintures: Scenes de la vie quotidienne.* Paris: A. and J. Picard, 1964, pl. 18, fig. 205 (left).

7. "Servant" Statues from the tomb of Ny-kau-inpu

   10618: Unpublished

   10635

   Breasted, James Henry, Jr. *Egyptian Servant Statues.* The Bollingen Series 13. New York: Pantheon Books, 1948, pp. 32–3, pl. 31b.

   Smith, William S. *History of Egyptian Sculpture and Painting in the Old Kingdom.* Second Edition. London: Oxford University Press, 1949, p. 97, pl. 28f.

   10628 (selected references)

   Arnold, Dorothea. *When the Pyramids were Built: Egyptian Art of the Old Kingdom.* New York: Metropolitan Museum of Art, 1999, pp. 110–11.

   Arnold, Dorothca and Christiane Ziegler (editors). *Egyptian Art in the Age of the Pyramids.* New York: Metropolitan Museum of Art, 1999, pp. 389–90, no. 138 A-B.

   Breasted, James Henry, Jr. *Egyptian Servant Statues.* The Bollingen Series 13. New York: Pantheon Books, 1948, pp. 49–50, pl. 45b.

   Hope, Colin. *Egyptian Pottery.* Shire Egyptology 5. Aylesbury: Shire, 1987, cover.

   L'art égyptien au temps des pyramides. Paris: Réunion des musées nationaux, 1999, p. 335, no. 164.

   Smith, William S. *History of Egyptian Sculpture and Painting in the Old Kingdom.* Second Edition. London: Oxford University Press, 1949, p. 100, pl. 28g.

   Vandier, Jacques. *Manuel d'archéologie égyptienne.* Vol. III. *Les Grandes Époques: La Statuaire.* Paris: A. and J. Picard, 1958, pl. XXXIX.

10641–2 (selected references)

Arnold, Dorothea and Christiane Ziegler (editors). *Egyptian Art in the Age of the Pyramids.* New York: Metropolitan Museum of Art, 1999, p. 391 (OIM 10641); p. 392 (OIM 10642).

Breasted, James Henry, Jr. *Egyptian Servant Statues.* The Bollingen Series 13. New York: Pantheon Books, 1948, pp. 86–87, pls. 80b, 81a-b.

Dasen, V. *Dwarfs in Ancient Egypt and Greece.* Oxford Monographs on Classical Archaeology. Oxford: Clarendon Press, 1993, pp. 40, 41, 122, 125, 277, pl. 29.

L'art égyptien au temps des pyramides. Paris: Réunion des musées nationaux, 1999, p. 339, no. 167.

Pérez, Arroya Rafael. *Egipto: La Música en la Era de las Pirámides.* Madrid: Ediciones Centro de Estudios Egipcios, 2000, pp. 312–14.

Smith, William S. *History of Egyptian Sculpture and Painting in the Old Kingdom.* Second edition. London: Oxford University Press, 1949, p. 101, pl. 27e.

Vandier, Jacques. *Manuel d'archéologie égyptienne.* Vol. III. *Les Grandes Époques: La Statuaire.* Paris: A. and J. Picard, 1958, pl. XL.

8. Nen-khefet-ka and his Wife Nefer-shemes 2036

Kanawati, N. and A. McFarlane. *Deshasha: The Tombs of Inti, Shedu and Others.* Reports 5. Sydney: The Australian Centre for Egyptology, 1993, pl. 61b (bottom, middle).

Petrie, W. M. Flinders. *Deshasheh.* Egypt Exploration Fund Memoir 15. London: The Egypt Exploration Fund, 1898, pp. 12–14, pl. XXXI.

Porter, Bertha and Rosalind Moss. *Topographical Bibliography of Ancient Egyptian Hieroglyphic Texts, Reliefs and Paintings.* Vol. IV: Lower and Middle Egypt (Delta and Cairo to Asyût). Oxford: Clarendon Press, 1934, p. 123.

Wilson, John. *The Burden of Egypt.* Chicago: University of Chicago Press, 1951, fig. 7c.

9. Lintel of Kha-bau-ptah 10815

Porter, Bertha and Rosalind Moss, *Topographical Bibliography of Ancient Egyptian Hieroglyphic Texts, Reliefs and Paintings,* Vol. III/2, Memphis, part 2: Saqqâra to Dahshûr. Oxford: Clarendon Press, 1981, p. 454.

10. A Warning to Tomb Robbers 10814

Porter, Bertha and Rosalind Moss, *Topographical Bibliography of Ancient Egyptian Hieroglyphic Texts, Reliefs and Paintings,* Vol. III/2, Memphis, part 2: Saqqâra to Dahshûr. Oxford: Clarendon Press, 1981, p. 677.

11. The Royal Herald, Neni 11489

Petrie, W. M. Flinders and Guy Brunton. *Sedment.* Vol. 1. British School of Archaeology in Egypt and Egyptian Research Account Publication 34. London: British School of Archaeology in Egypt, 1924, p. 4, pl. 1, nos. 19–21.

12. Uha and his Wife Henut-sen 16956

Bailey, Susan. "Circumcision and Male Initiation." In *Egypt in Africa*, edited by Theodore Celenko. Indianapolis: Indianapolis Museum of Art, 1996, pp. 89–90.

Cherpion, Nadine. "Sentiment Conjugal et Figuration à l'Ancien Empire." In *Kunst des Alten Reiches*, edited by Rainer Stadelmann and Hourig Sourouzian. Mainz: Philipp von Zabern, 1995, p. 35, pl. 6b.

Dunham, Dows. *Naga-ed-Dêr Stelae of the First Intermediate Period.* Boston: Museum of Fine Arts, 1937, pp. 102–4, pl. XXXII.

Wilson, John. *The Burden of Egypt.* Chicago: University of Chicago Press, 1951, fig. 11a.

13. Model Workshop 11495

Breasted, James Henry, Jr. *Egyptian Servant Statues.* Washington, D.C.: Pantheon Books, 1948, p. 40, pl. 40a.

Marfoe, Leon. *A Guide to the Oriental Institute Museum.* Chicago: The Oriental Institute, 1982, p. 36.

Petrie, W. M. Flinders and Guy Brunton. *Sedment.* Vol. 1. British School of Archaeology in Egypt and Egyptian Research Account Publication 34. London: British School of Archaeology in Egypt, 1924, p. 10, pl. XVI, no. 374.

14. A Letter to the Dead 13945

   Gardiner, Alan H. "A New Letter to the Dead." *Journal of Egyptian Archaeology* 16 (1930): 19–22.

15. Stela of the Household of Senbu 6739

   Garstang, John. *El Arábah: A Cemetery of the Middle Kingdom; Survey of the Old Kingdom Temenos; Graffiti from the Temple of Sety.* Egyptian Research Account Sixth Memoir. London: School of Archaeology in Egypt/Bernard Quaritch, 1900, pp. 33, 41, 46, pl. XII, lower right.

16. Nakht and Seth-Antewy 10510

   Cartwright, Harry. "The Iconography of Certain Egyptian Divinities as Illustrated by Collections in the Oriental Institute Museum." *American Journal of Semitic Languages and Literature* 45 (April, 1929): 185.

   Gardiner, Alan H. *Ancient Egyptian Onomastica.* Vol. II. Oxford: Oxford University Press, 1947, pp. 53*–54*, 62*–64*.

   te Velde, Herman. *Seth, God of Confusion.* Probleme der Ägyptologie 6. Leiden: E. J. Brill, 1977, p. 68, pl. IV.1.

17. Funerary Figure of Kenamun 25648

   Oriental Institute News & Notes. No. 100. September-October 1985, pp. 8–9.

18. Child's Tunic 18285

   Unpublished

19. Statue of a God 10607

   Kozloff, Arielle, Betsy Bryan with Lawrence Berman (editors). *Egypt's Dazzling Sun: Amenhotep III and his World.* Cleveland: Cleveland Art Museum, 1992, pp. 178–81.

   Marfoe, Leon. *A Guide to the Oriental Institute Museum.* Chicago: The Oriental Institute, 1982, p. 34, fig. 21.

   Vandier, Jacques. *Manuel d'archéologie égyptienne.* Vol. III, *Les Grandes Époques: La Statuaire.* Paris: A and J. Picard, 1958, pl. CXXIII.6, p. 384.

   Wilson, John. *The Burden of Egypt.* Chicago: University of Chicago Press, 1951, fig. 7b.

20. Game of Twenty Squares 371

   Marfoe, Leon. *A Guide to the Oriental Institute Museum.* Chicago: The Oriental Institute, 1982, p. 31, fig. 19.

21. Detail of a Funerary Procession 11047

   Polz, Daniel. *Das Grab des Hui und des Kel, Theban Nr. 54.* Archäologische Veröffentlichungen 74. Mainz: Philipp von Zabern, 1997, pp. 35–36, pls. 8, 17.

   Silverman, David. "A New Kingdom Funerary Ritual and Procession." *Serapis* 6 (1980): 125–33.

22. Running Ibexes 11398

   Unpublished

23. Colossal Statue of Tutankhamun 14088 (Selected references)

   Forbes, Dennis. "Tutankhamen on the Move at Chicago's Oriental Institute Museum." *KMT*, vol. 9, no. 3, (Fall 1998): 30–33.

   Gabolde, Marc. *Le Père Ay, Corpus commenté des documents et état questions.* Ph.D. dissertation, University of Lyon, 1992, pp. 136–9.

   Hölscher, Uvo. *The Excavation of Medinet Habu.* Vol. 2. *The Temples of the Eighteenth Dynasty.* Oriental Institute Publications 41. Chicago: University of Chicago Press, 1939, pp. 102–4, pls. 44–47.

   Hölscher, Uvo. *Excavations at Ancient Thebes 1930/31.* Oriental Institute Communications 15. Chicago: University of Chicago Press, 1932, pp. 50–53.

   Murnane, William. "Featured Object Number 5: Colossal Statue of Tutankhamun from West Thebes (Oriental Institute 14088)." Chicago: The Oriental Institute, n.d.

   Teeter, Emily. "Restored Colossus of Tutankhamun." *Amarna Letters* 2. San Francisco: KMT Communications, 1992, pp. 87–91.

   Wilson, Karen and Joan Barghusen. *Highlights of the Collection.* Chicago: The Oriental Institute, 1989, no. 18.

24. Amun 10503

Peck, William. "A Seated Statue of Amun." *Journal of Egyptian Archaeology* 57 (1971): 74–5.

25. Seti I and Ramesses II 10507

Habachi, Labib. "La reine Touy, femme de Séthi I, et ses proches parents inconnus." *Revue d'Égyptologie* 21 (1969): pp. 45–46 [8], pl. 3.

Kitchen, Kenneth. *Ramesside Inscriptions*. Vol. 1. Oxford: Blackwell, 1975, p. 320.

Martin, Geoffrey. *Corpus of Reliefs of the New Kingdom from the Memphite Necropolis and Lower Egypt*. Vol 1. London: KPI, 1987, pp. 30–31 [no. 74], pl. 27.

Martin, Geoffrey. *The Tomb of Tia and Tia: A Royal Monument of the Ramesside Period in the Memphite Necropolis*. Egypt Exploration Fund Memoir 58. London: Egypt Exploration Society, 1997, pp. 47–8, 49–51, 54, pl. 98.

26. Two Scenes of Nature 16879, 16880

Unpublished

27. The Bad Boy 13951 (Selected references)

Breasted, James Henry. *The Oriental Institute*. Chicago: University of Chicago, 1933, p. 424, fig. 206.

Brovarski, Edward, Susan Doll, and Rita Freed (editors). *Egypt's Golden Age: The Art of Living in the New Kingdom 1558–1085 B.C.* Boston: Museum of Fine Arts, 1982, p. 279, no. 382.

Brunner-Traut, Emma. "Ägyptische Tiermärchen." *Zeitschrift für ägyptische Sprache und Altertumskunde* 80 (1955): 24 (no. 25), pl. 2.1.

——————. *Altägyptische Tiergeschichte und Fabel*. Darmstadt: Wissenschaftliche Buchgesellschaft, 1968, p. 14, fig. 9 (with boy's phallus erased).

Janssen, Rosalind and Jack Janssen. *Egyptian Household Animals*. Shire Egyptology 12. Aylesbury: Shire Publications, 1989, p. 61, fig. 51.

Peck, William and John Ross. *Egyptian Drawings*. New York: Dutton, 1978, p. 78, no. 77.

Marfoe, Leon. *A Guide to the Oriental Institute Museum*. Chicago: The Oriental Institute, 1982, p. 25, fig. 13.

Wilson, John. *The Burden of Egypt*. Chicago: University of Chicago, 1951, fig. 16a.

28. Stela Dedicated to the God Reshep 10569 (Selected references)

Fulco, W. J. *The Canaanite God Rešep*. American Oriental Series 8. New Haven: American Oriental Society, 1976, pp. 14–15.

Pritchard, James. *The Ancient Near East in Pictures Relating to the Old Testament*. Princeton: Princeton University Press, 1969, p. 164, no. 475.

Schulman, Alan. "The Winged Reshep." *The Journal of the American Research Center in Egypt* 16 (1979): 76, no. 11.

Simpson, William. "Reschef," In *Lexikon der Ägyptologie*, edited by Wolfgang Helck, Vol. V. Wiesbaden: Otto Harrassowitz, 1984, col. 245.

Stadelmann, Rainer. *Syrische-Palästinenische Gottheiten in Ägypten*. Probleme der Ägyptologie 5. Leiden: E. J. Brill, 1967, p. 70.

Vernus, Pascal. *Athribis*. Bibliothèque d'Étude 74. Cairo: Institut français d'archéologie orientale du Caire, 1978, pp. 56–7.

29. Decorative Tiles 16672, 16721

Hayes, William. *Glazed Tiles from a Palace of Ramesses II at Kantir*. New York: The Metropolitan Museum, 1937, pp. 22, 27, 32.

16672

Hölscher. Uvo. *The Excavation of Medinet Habu*. Vol. IV. *The Mortuary Temple of Ramses II, Part II*. Oriental Institute Publications 55. Chicago: University of Chicago Press, 1955, pp. 41–2, 44 (35g), pls. 5, 35g.

16721

Hölscher. Uvo. *The Excavation of Medinet Habu*. Vol. IV. *The Mortuary Temple of Ramses II, Part II*. Oriental Institute Publications 55. Chicago: University of Chicago Press, 1955, pp. 41–2,44 (35c), pls. 5, 35c, 38d.

30. Floral Column 14089

   Handbook of the Oriental Institute. Fourth Edition. Chicago: University of Chicago Press, 1935, fig. 16, p. 20.

   Hölscher, Uvo. *Excavation of Medinet Habu.* Vol. IV. *The Mortuary Temple of Ramses III, Part II.* Oriental Institute Publications 55. Chicago: University of Chicago Press, 1955, pp. 9–10, pl. 4 (right).

   Nelson, Harold and Uvo Hölscher. *Work in Western Thebes 1931–33.* Oriental Institute Communications 18. Chicago: University of Chicago Press, 1934, pp. 95–99, fig. 53 (right).

31. Grooming Implements

   10582: Hughes, George. "The Cosmetic Arts in Ancient Egypt." *The Journal of the Society of Cosmetic Chemists* 10 (1959): 174–75, fig. 7.

   Other objects unpublished

32. Study for a Royal Tomb Painting 17006

   Van Siclen, Charles. "A Ramesside Ostracon of Queen Isis." *Journal of Near Eastern Studies* 33 (1974): 150–53.

33. Head of a King 15554

   Brewer, Douglas and Emily Teeter. *Egypt and the Egyptians.* Cambridge: Cambridge University Press, 1999, p. 173, fig. 11.2.

34. Canopic Jars 2091–2094
   Unpublished

35. A Priest of Hathor 10729

   Ritner, Robert. "Denderite Temple Hierarchy and the Family of the Theban High Priest Nebwenenef: Block Statue OIM 10729." In *For His Ka: Essays Offered in Memory of Klaus Baer,* edited by David P. Silverman. Studies in Ancient Oriental Civilization 55. Chicago: The Oriental Institute, 1994, pp. 205–26.

36. Stela of the Hearing Ear 16718

   Teeter, Emily. "Hearing Ear Stela." In *The American Discovery of Ancient Egypt,* edited by Nancy Thomas, Vol. 1. Los Angeles: Los Angeles Museum of Art, 1995, p. 193.

37. Offering to the God 1351 (Selected references)

   Lichtheim, Miriam. "Situla No. 11395 and Some Remarks on Egyptian Situlae." *Journal of Near Eastern Studies* 6 (1947): 174, pl. VIIA.

   Quibell, James. *The Ramesseum.* Egypt Exploration Fund Memoir 2. London: The Egyptian Exploration Fund, 1896, pp. 11, 17, pl. XX.4.

   Teeter, Emily. "Popular Worship in Ancient Egypt." *KMT* (Summer, 1993), cover.

   Wilson, Karen and Joan Barghusen. *Highlights from the Collection.* Chicago: The Oriental Institute, 1989, no. 2.

38. Cartonnage Case and Mummy of Meresamun 10797

   Teeter, Emily. "The Mummy and Coffin of Meresamun." Featured Object Number 9. Published on the Oriental Institute Home Page (electronic publication), 1996.

39. Brick Stamp 11171
   Unpublished

40. Amunirdis I and Diese-heb-sed 14681

   Teeter, Emily. "Diese-hebsed, A *ḥst ẖnw n Imn* at Medinet Habu," *Varia Aegyptiaca* 10, nos. 2–3 (August–December 1995): 195–203.

41. Reliefs from the Tomb of Montuemhet 17973–5, 18828 (selected references)

   Bothmer, Bernard (editor). *Egyptian Sculpture of the Late Period.* Brooklyn: The Brooklyn Museum, 1960, pp. 17–18 (no. 15), pl. 14, fig. 33.

Der Manuelian, Peter. "An Essay in Reconstruction: Two Registers from the Tomb of Mentuemhat at Thebes (no. 34)." *Mitteilungen des Deutschen Archäologischen Instituts, Abteilung Kairo* 39 (1983): 131–50.

Kantor, Helene. "A Fragment of Relief from the Tomb of Montuemhet at Thebes (No. 34)." *Journal of Near Eastern Studies* 19 (1960): 213–16.

Russmann, Edna. "Relief Decoration in the Tomb of Mentuemhat (TT 34)." *Journal of the American Research Center in Egypt* 31 (1994): 13, no. 72.

42. Statue of Amun 10584

De Meulenaere, Herman. "La famille du roi Amasis." *Journal of Egyptian Archaeology* 54 (1968): 186–87, pl. XXIX 2–3.

43. Stela of Harsiese 12220 (Selected references)

Allen, Thomas George. *The Egyptian Book of the Dead: Documents in the Oriental Institute Museum at the University of Chicago.* Oriental Institute Publications 82. Chicago: University of Chicago Press, 1960, pp. 12, 13, 60, 80, 82, pl. CIII.

Brewer, Douglas and Emily Teeter. *Egypt and the Egyptians.* Cambridge: Cambridge University Press, 1999, cover.

Munro, Peter. *Die spätägyptischen Totenstelen.* Ägyptologische Forschungen 25. Glückstadt: J. J. Augustin, 1973, p. 196.

44. Donation Stela 13943

Leahy, Anthony. "Two Donation Stelae of Necho II." *Revue d' Égyptologie* 34 (1982–3): 84–91.

Meeks, Dimitri. "Les donations aux temples dans l'Égypte du Ier millénaire avant J.-C." In *State and Temple Economy in the Ancient Near East,* edited by Edward Lipiński. Orientalia Lovaniensia Analecta 5–6. Leuven: Department Oriëntalistiek, 1979, p. 676 (26.2.11).

Morschauser, Scott. *Threat Formulae in Ancient Egypt.* Baltimore: Halgo, 1991, p. 10.

45. Composite Deity 11375

Cartwright, Harry. "The Iconography of Certain Egyptian Divinities as Illustrated by Collections in the Oriental Institute Museum." *American Journal of Semitic Languages and Literature* 45 (April, 1929): 196, fig. 28.

Teeter, Emily."Animals in Egyptian Religion." In *A History of the Animal World in the Ancient Near East,* edited by Billie Jean Collins. Leiden: Brill, 2002, p. 354, fig. 12.7.

46. Demotic "Marriage" Papyrus 17481

Jasnow, Richard. *Oriental Institute Hawara Papyri: Demotic and Greek Texts from an Egyptian Family Archive in the Fayum (Fourth to Third Centuries B.C.).* Oriental Institute Publications 113. Chicago: The Oriental Institute, 1997, pp. 3–4, 7, 9–15, pls. 1–7.

Nims, Charles. "A Demotic 'Document of Endowment' from the Time of Nectanebo I." *Mitteilungen des Deutschen Archäologischen Instituts, Abteilung Kairo* 16 (1958): 237–46.

47. Head from a Cat Coffin 18826

Unpublished

48. Oracular Statue in the Form of a Falcon 10504 (Selected references)

Bothmer, Bernard. "The Nodding Falcon of the Guennol Collection at the Brooklyn Museum." The *Brooklyn Museum Annual IX* (1967–1968): 75–76.

Marfoe, Leon. *A Guide to the Oriental Institute Museum.* Chicago: The Oriental Institute, 1982, p. 23, fig. 11.

Wilson, Karen and Joan Barghusen. *Highlights from the Collection.* Chicago: The Oriental Institute, 1989, no. 14.

49. Thoth Emblem 10101

Unpublished

50. Ritual Vessel (Situla) 11394

Unpublished

51. Book of the Dead 9787

Allen, Thomas George. *Book of the Dead: Documents in the Oriental Institute Museum at the University of Chicago.* Oriental Institute Publications 82. Chicago: University of Chicago Press, 1960, pp. 10, 16–39, 202–03, pls. 34–35 (pls. 13–50 for entire papyrus).

52. Statue Base of Djed-hor 10589

Sherman, Elizabeth. "Djedḥor the Saviour Statue Base OI 10589." *Journal of Egyptian Archaeology* 67 (1981): 82–102, pls. XIII–XIV.

Vernus, Pascal. *Athribis*. Bibliothèque d'Étude 74. Cairo: Institut français d'archéologie orientale du Caire, 1978, p. 196, doc. 162.

Young, Eric. "A Possible Consanguinous Marriage in the Time of Philip Arrhidaeus." *Journal of the American Research Center in Egypt* 4 (1965): 69–71.

53. Horus on the Crocodiles 16881 (Selected references)

Seele, Keith. "Oriental Institute Museum Notes: Horus on the Crocodiles." *Journal of Near Eastern Studies* 6 (1947): 43–52.

Sternberg-El Hotabi, Heike. *Untersuchungen zur Überlieferungsgeschichte der Horrusstelen*. Vol. 1. Ägyptologische Abhandlungen 62. Wiesbaden: Otto Harrassowitz, 1999, pp. 107, 110, fig. 56.

Teeter, Emily. "Animals in Egyptian Religion." In *A History of the Animal World in the Ancient Near East*, edited by Billie Jean Collins. Leiden: Brill, 2002, p. 353, fig. 12.6.

54. Cult Statue of Queen Arsinoe II 10518 (Selected references)

Fraser, P. M. "Inscriptions from Ptolemaic Egypt." *Berytus* 13 no. 2 (1959–60): 133–4, pl. XXIX 2 a–b.

Fraser, P. M. *Ptolemaic Alexandria*. Vol. 1. Oxford: The Clarendon Press, 1972, p. 70, no. 234.

Quaegebeur, Jan. "Documents égyptiens anciens et nouveaux relatifs à Arsinoé Philadelphe." In *Le cult du souverain dans l'Égypte ptolémaïque au IIIe siècle avant notre ère*, edited by H. Melaerts. Louvain: Peeters, 1998, p. 89, no. 3.

Quaegebeur, Jan. "Ptolémée II en adoration devant Arsinoé II divinisée." *Bulletin de l'Institut français d'archéologie orientale* 69 (1971): 210, no. 5.

Stanwick, Paul. *Portraits of the Ptolemies: Greek Kings as Egyptian Pharaohs*. Austin: University of Texas Press, 2002, pp. 25, 38, 39, 56, 68, 100–01.

55. Water Clock (Clepsydra) 16875

Quaegebeur, Jan. "Documents Concerning a Cult of Arsinoe Philadelphos at Memphis." *Journal of Near Eastern Studies* 30 (1971): 259–62, 270, pls. 2–3.

56. Relief Fragment 19517

Oriental Institute Annual Report 1961–62, Chicago: The Oriental Institute, pp. 23–4.

57. Sandal 7189

Unpublished

58. Mummy Mask 7177

Unpublished

59. Funerary Stela of Pa-sher-o-pehty 5116

Petrie, W. M. Flinders. *Dendereh 1898*. Seventeenth Memoir. London: The Egypt Exploration Fund, 1900, p. 55, no. XVI.

60. Mummy Portrait 2053

Unpublished

61. Mask from a Funerary Shroud 9385

Riggs, Christine. "Roman Period Mummy Masks from Deir el Bahari." *Journal of Egyptian Archaeology* 86 (2000): 143 n. 17.

62. Lamp in the Form of a Bird 16734

Hölscher, Uvo. *The Excavation of Medinet Habu*. Vol. V. *Post Ramessid Remains*. Oriental Institute Publications 66. Chicago: University of Chicago Press, 1954, p. 64, pl. 38:4.

Wilfong, T. G. Brochure for exhibit "Another Egypt: Coptic Christians at Thebes (7th–8th centuries A.D.)." Chicago: The Oriental Institute, 1990, cover.

4. CHRONOLOGY

All dates before 664 B.C. are approximate. When dynasties overlap, each controlled a different part of Egypt. When rulers overlap within a dynasty, two kings shared power. Only selected kings are listed for each dynasty. This chronology is based, in part, upon Jürgen von Beckerath's *Chronologie des pharaonischen Ägypten*.

PREDYNASTIC PERIOD	**CA. 5000 B.C.–3100 B.C.**
EARLY DYNASTIC PERIOD	**DYNASTIES 1–2 CA. 3100–2707 B.C.**
Dynasty 1	3100–2853 B.C.
Dynasty 2	2853–2707 B.C.
OLD KINGDOM	**DYNASTIES 3–6 CA. 2707–2219 B.C.**
Dynasty 3	2707–2639 B.C.
Huni	2663–2639 B.C.
Dynasty 4	2639–2504 B.C.
Snefru	2639–2604 B.C.
Khufu (Cheops)	2604–2581 B.C.
Khafre (Chephren)	2572–2546 B.C.
Menkaure (Mycerinus)	2539–2511 B.C.
Dynasty 5	2504–2347 B.C.
Userkaf	2504–2496 B.C.
Sahure	2496–2483 B.C.
Neferirkare	2483–2463 B.C.
Niuserre	2445–2414 B.C.
Menkauhor	2414–2405 B.C.
Unas	2367–2347 B.C.
Dynasty 6	2347–2216 B.C.
Teti	2347–2337 B.C.
Pepi I	2335–2285 B.C.
Pepi II	2279–2219 B.C.
FIRST INTERMEDIATE PERIOD	**DYNASTIES 7–11 CA. 2219–1995 B.C.**
Dynasty 7	2219–2219? B.C.
Dynasty 8	2216–2107 B.C.
Dynasties 9–10	2170–2025 B.C.
Dynasty 11	2119–1976 B.C.
Mentuhotep II	2046–1995 B.C.

MIDDLE KINGDOM	DYNASTIES 11–13 CA. 1995–1648 B.C.
Dynasty 12	1976–1794 B.C.
Dynasty 13	1794–1648 B.C.

SECOND INTERMEDIATE PERIOD	DYNASTIES 14–17 CA. 1720–1550 B.C.
Dynasty 14	1720?–1648 B.C.
Dynasty 15	1648–1539 B.C.
Dynasty 16	1648–1539 B.C.
Dynasty 17	1645–1550 B.C.

NEW KINGDOM	DYNASTIES 18–20 CA. 1550–1070 B.C.
Dynasty 18	1550–1292 B.C.
Amunhotep I	1526–1505 B.C.
Thutmose I	1505–1492 B.C.
Thutmose II	1492–1479 B.C.
Thutmose III	1479–1425 B.C.
Hatshepsut	1473–1458 B.C.
Amunhotep II	1428–1400 B.C.
Thutmose IV	1400–1390 B.C.
Amunhotep III	1390–1353 B.C.
Amunhotep IV–Akhenaten	1352–1336 B.C.
Smenkhkare	1336–1334 B.C.
Tutankhamun	1334–1325 B.C.
Aye	1325–1321 B.C.
Horemhab	1321–1292 B.C.
Dynasty 19	1292–1856 B.C.
Ramesses I	1293–1291 B.C.
Seti I	1291–1279 B.C.
Ramesses II	1279–1212 B.C.
Merenptah	1212–1202 B.C.
Dynasty 20	1186–1070 B.C.
Ramesses III	1182–1151 B.C.
Ramesses VI	1142–1134 B.C.

THIRD INTERMEDIATE PERIOD	**DYNASTIES 21-25 CA. 1070-664 B.C.**
Dynasty 21	1070–946 b.c.
Dynasty 22	946–735 B.C.
Shoshenq II	877–875 B.C.
Dynasty 23	756–714 B.C.
Dynasty 24	740–714 B.C.
Dynasty 25 (Nubian)	746–664 B.C.
Piye (Piankhy)	746–715 B.C.
LATE PERIOD	**DYNASTIES 26-31 664-332 B.C.**
Dynasty 26	664–525 B.C.
Psamtik I	664–610 B.C
Necho II	610–595 B.C.
Psamtik II	595–589 B.C.
Apries	589–570 B.C.
Amasis	570–526 B.C.
Psamtik II	526–525 B.C.
Dynasty 27 (First Persian Period)	525–401 B.C.
Dynasty 28	404–399 B.C.
Dynasty 29	399–380 B.C.
Dynasty 30	380–342 B.C.
Nectanebo I	380–362 B.C.
Nectanebo II	360–343 B.C.
Dynasty 31 (Second Persian Period)	342–332 B.C.
Darius III	335–332 B.C.
MACEDONIAN KINGS	**332-305 B.C.**
Alexander the Great	332–323 B.C.
Philip Arrhidaeus	323–317 B.C.
PTOLEMAIC PERIOD	**305-30 B.C.**
Ptolemy I	305–284 B.C.
Ptolemy II	284–246 B.C.
Cleopatra VII	51–30 B.C.
ROMAN PERIOD	**30 B.C.-337 A.D.**
BYZANTINE (COPTIC) PERIOD	**4TH-7TH CENTURIES A.D.**

5. MAP

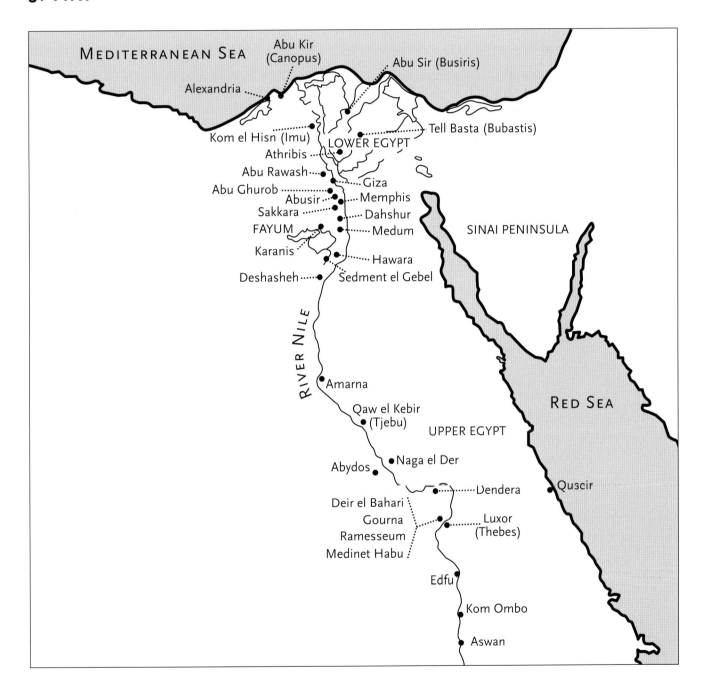

MEDITERRANEAN SEA

Abu Kir (Canopus)

Abu Sir (Busiris)

Alexandria

Kom el Hisn (Imu)

Tell Basta (Bubastis)

LOWER EGYPT

Athribis

Abu Rawash

Giza

Abu Ghurob

Memphis

Abusir

Sakkara

Dahshur

FAYUM

Medum

Karanis

Hawara

Deshasheh

Sedment el Gebel

SINAI PENINSULA

RIVER NILE

RED SEA

Amarna

Qaw el Kebir (Tjebu)

UPPER EGYPT

Naga el Der

Abydos

Dendera

Quseir

Deir el Bahari

Gourna

Luxor (Thebes)

Ramesseum

Medinet Habu

Edfu

Kom Ombo

Aswan

INDICES

GENERAL INDEX

ANCIENT EGYPTIAN ROYAL NAMES

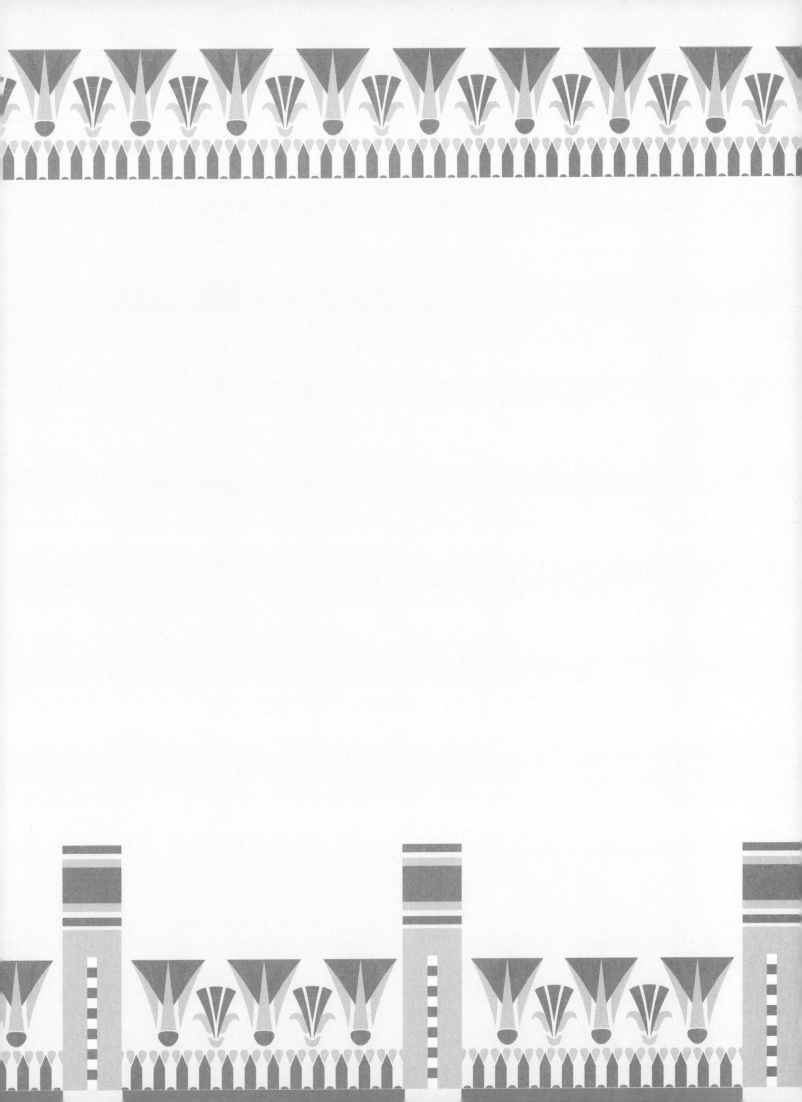

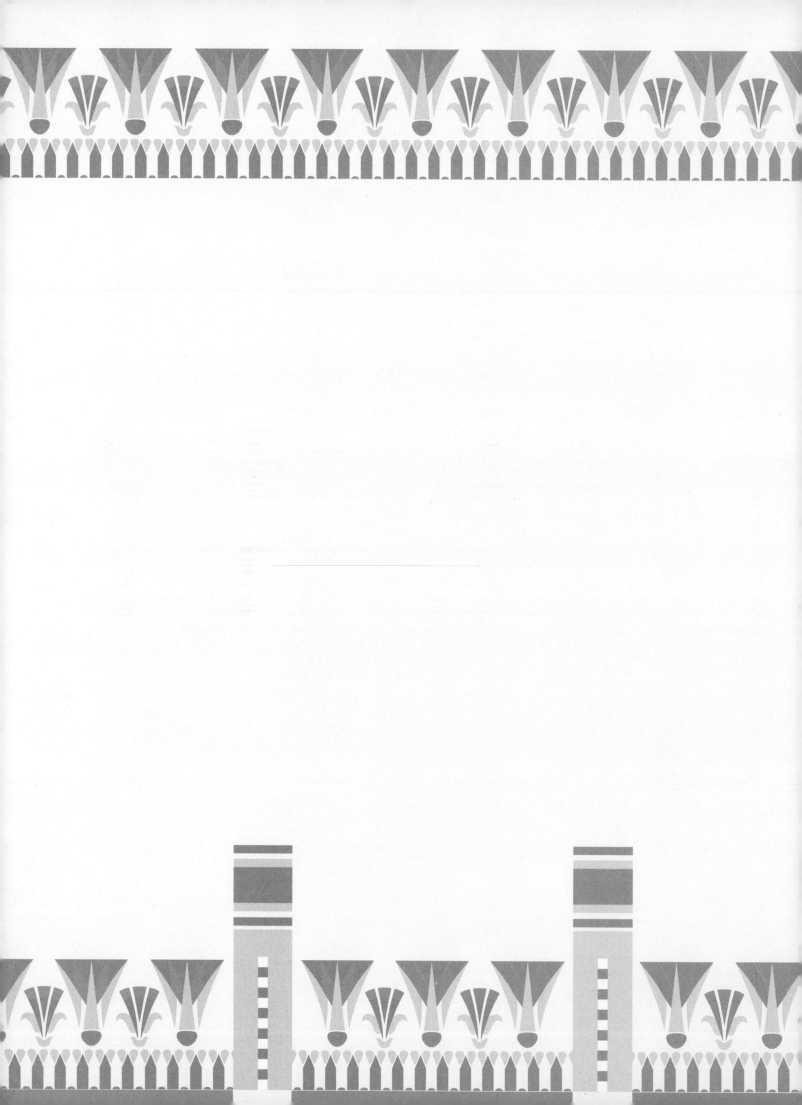